RELEASE THE BATS

WRITING YOUR WAY OUT OF IT

DBC PIERRE

FABER & FABER

First published in the UK in 2016
by Faber & Faber Limited
Bloomsbury House,
74–77 Great Russell Street, London WC1B 3DA

Typeset by Faber & Faber Limited
Printed in the UK by CPI Group (UK) Ltd, Croydon, CR0 4YY

A CIP record for this book
is available from the British Library

ISBN 978–0–571–28318–7

2 4 6 8 10 9 7 5 3 1

For prisoners everywhere.
Which also means us.

CONTENTS

PART ONE
Writing: As Exciting as Burglary

PART TWO
Going Equipped

PART THREE
Toolbox

APPENDIX
Quick Guide

It's none of their business that you have to learn to write. Let them think you were born that way.

Ernest Hemingway

SPUR

I went to Tegel prison in Berlin one Thursday. Its full name, *Justizvollzugsanstalt Tegel*, paints the picture of gunmetal sky over red-brick walls. Officers frisked me and traded my passport and belongings for a token which they warned me not to lose. The driver who brought me declined to come in: he was once a detective who had put some inmates away. I was going to read and chat with a writing group made up of long-term prisoners. My prison host said they would find the talk interesting, but not as compelling as the last two minutes of our time. When the official talk was over there would be a gap before guards came to lock everyone up. In those couple of minutes the prisoners would mingle and meet someone fresh.

That time was gold for them.

When the time came it was a fleeting party without drinks, of conversation between men close together. Ice had to be broken fast, years of isolation charged to moments no longer than a traffic-light change. In that time one of the men came asking me serious questions. His writing had hit a snag: he'd been inside so long that he'd forgotten what the streets outside were like. He couldn't imagine the world enough, its dynamics and feel, to write a recognisable setting. And he had no access to the internet. I realised what a pure canvas the prisoners were facing as writers.

I could tell this was the first of many questions from the man. My heart was in my throat. I started to tell him that in some ways we're all trapped away from the truth or detail of what we try to write; but before I could explain, guards appeared at both our sides and physically pulled us apart.

What follows is the rest of my answers.

NUTSHELL

You can be insecure and be a writer.

You can be unsuccessful and be a writer.

You can be a bad person and be a writer.

You can be a drinker, a procrastinator, a freak.

You can be compulsive, dependent, delusional, manic.

You can be under house arrest.

You can be on medication.

You can be wrong.

And be a writer.

You just have to write.

That's where it gets tricky.

There are a million gurus, books and groups that can tell you where the verb goes, and sell you a rewarding, methodical way to write.

This book is about another way.

One you might end up with.

Because once you get over this being a job you can do in your underwear you will find yourself in that underwear in the dead of some miserable night more alone than you thought you could be.

And you won't give a fuck where the verb goes.

PREFACE

I started to write. It wasn't a lifelong wish. I didn't train for it, didn't know any writers, editors or publishers. I just had a strong feeling with nowhere to go.

I wasn't particularly well-read, though I loved books and carried some more vividly in mind than real life. I had imagination, could speak my native tongue and talk shit about art. Against that, Shakespeare was still in the shops and the streets were full of graduates. Long-odds schemes were rarely lucky for me, and writing blind seemed long odds. Still, the feeling smouldered till I had nothing to lose, till there was just the two of us; then it caught a spark and ignited. A new climate took hold with its own laws, a place where Douglas Adams' art of flying was key, the art of throwing yourself at the ground and missing. The trick was in missing.

Thankfully it's a knack you can practise over time. When you first sit down to write, a hundred thousand decisions glare up from blank pages. They grow as you frown, and must be the reason most books are never written. Not that the decisions can't be made, but you have to make them alone and from scratch. They're all your fault, and their sum effect is your fault. But a curious thing can also happen: as you ponder how dumb it is to risk getting that many decisions right, you can end up feeling that alone, and from scratch is where writing wants you. Where it wants every writer. That the risk is the whole job. That hauling you naked to a place where nobody can help you is how writing wrings out art. That the management of passion counts as much as the words, and that every new book should make its author a novice again.

Which, as a novice, makes you a writer.

The only matter then is to keep writing.

For me at first it was like trying to paint a dictionary onto live rats, but the more naked and clueless I grew, the more power I found, and it was correct. The gods of writing weren't waiting for another impeccable tome from some learned technician, they were waiting for a shout from the rooftops. For mine and for yours. My feeling was that shout and by isolating it, wrestling it, and building it a cage, I was harnessing the only thing I had to give. I couldn't compete with theory or craft, the shout was all I had. But take note if you mean to write: it was enough. Had I been guided by an editor, tutor or group, I wouldn't have written what I wrote. There was no way to explain the feeling, even to myself. The novel is its only explanation.

This book is my guide to, and reflection on, that job. Clearly there are many more qualified people than me for this, but I didn't know any of those people when I started to write, and almost none have published clues for stragglers. I didn't want the PhD course, just a few good keys; and while there's a great deal more to be said about writing than is here, I can also now honestly say that the practical secrets to a page-turning book would easily fit onto a napkin. I'll spread them more liberally, but you get the idea. If you want to write a spy novel, the formula is in Part Three and takes up a fraction of these pages. This book is longer because the formula is the easy part: getting ourselves to sit at a table long enough to write a book is the tricky part, plus writing the damn book. I'm not a teacher but maybe it's for the best, I only include what made itself noticeable along the way. Whether it breaks rules or is noticeable to others, I wouldn't know. This isn't about life as the writers we can become, disciplined and with our own routines, it's about breaking through. Think of it as a notebook from someone a day ahead of you on the same hunt. If you're writing it's about missing the ground. If you're a reader it's about the strange ecology of people, ideas and words. If you're a maniac it's a decoy for demons.

Maniacs are in good company. It turns out that demons are gatekeepers of literature. Books not only explore human weaknesses but are written in spite of them, are even inspired and driven by them. In this way they're organic, an honest book is human tissue. In trying to make this one of them I'm hoping these chapters also bring a change of perspective; not just a discussion but a day-trip to a viewpoint as we read. It can take an effort to see life through fresh eyes, and as the book is about fostering new sight it should try to provoke it along the way. Apart from anything, our biases and opinions are increasingly shaped by outside forces, we have to look beyond them more than ever to see things as they really are. Behind that shorthand of convenient ideas there's a playground for writers where things still sparkle with paradox, where few characters live down to their stereotypes, where the assailant can also be soft, the victim bad, the terrorist poetic. Anywhere uncomfortable ideas roam, ones that go against conditioned thought, is a mine for us; and wherever we sense that discomfort we find precisely the issues needing light. When we see topics put beyond argument, as so many now are, we find the ones that need it most, the ones whose rational claims probably don't support them, hence their quarantine in some taboo. Not to say we should all set out to write prickly books, nor that conditioned ideas are necessarily false; just that expected reality is often more fictional than good fiction, and we need to know which is which. Our workspace is between them. We have the privilege of writing life as it is, which can make our work glisten with truth. Everyone recognises a lurking fact when they see one, and literature is the last public space where we can expose them without influence from money or politics. Throughout history one has only had to say the truth to be subversive, and that has never been more true than today.

That it's a shrinking arena should owe nothing to us.

Although centuries of scholarship tell us what writing is and should be, and I can't pretend to expand on that, what I can do is share some things I wish I'd known in the dead of certain nights. Sure, they're subjective and idiosyncratic. But life's an experiment, I measure and observe it, and I watched this little odyssey like a hawk. In these chapters I might seem more of an evangelist or a drug dealer than a writer, and I apologise if it detracts from the mundane grind of writing, because it is also a grind – but like a moth between lights it's my nature to commute between dirt and sky, looking back from in between to see what I missed. I feel there's something helpful in it, but it's an outsider's place, neither here nor there; and that's where we'll go to write. Whatever form turns you on, short or long, fiction or non, the nuts, bolts and secrets are easier to grasp than you might think, and I include them here. It's all the other shit you'll find unexpected. However it is, I consign the whole mess to you in as bracing and useful a form as I can think of – like a bottle to swig from in your own dead of night.

DBC Pierre, London

HOW TO USE THIS BOOK

You don't have to be thinking of writing to read this book. I even hope you're not, then at least one of us is getting some sleep. Unlike literary fiction, where I get to please myself, with this book I have to imagine who might be reading. As I see it's you, I'll try to start most of these chapters with a moral anecdote – a scene – which I hope you'll enjoy with freedom one day in a park some-where. But if you're thinking of writing, those scenes are examples from life that relate to a second part in most chapters – a sequel – where their connection to writing is explored.

At the end of the book I'll list the bare nuts and bolts in an appendix. If you rip those pages out and paste them over your wall they should map all you need to know. I still write, so we can do this together. I warn you now that some of us won't make it. But some of us will – and to you who do: mine's a tequila.

PART ONE
WRITING: AS EXCITING AS BURGLARY

A state of mind in anguished conflict between a palpitating impulse to communicate and a profound distrust of my own adequacy.

Thomas Mann, *Doctor Faustus*

1 WHY ME

For over twenty years my mother drove on a forged foreign driving licence. I was the forger. I did it at school, probably in maths. She could drive well enough but couldn't work out the diagrams in written tests. So it was a technicality, which made it all right. It was one of many ways in which creativity was fostered at home, and things were made all right. Home was big and patrolled by people who always said 'yes' because they were under our employ. A closed circuit where whims could roam free. My father had better things to do than mess with it. Like all closed circuits it was a safe and constant environment – for as long as the circuit stayed closed.

I say it to identify two things that led to me writing:

The first is the difference in values between my house and the world outside. Granted, we're all raised in moral micro-climates to some degree, where the Johnsons are slippery because they now claim we never loaned them that book, and it's OK to tell everyone we're away for the weekend – but the degree to which our climate tallies with outside standards makes it noticeable to us or not, looking back.

Looking back, mine was like a neon motel sign. When my father's death broke the circuit, all that colour fizzed onto the street, so that whereas a boy ideally leaves home to trim his ideas to a wider breeze, I went into the world to have mine kicked out of me like seven kinds of shit. Which in itself is no good for writing. What's good is having to reappraise things from scratch. I had to study the gap between values, which meant learning where they came from and what was behind them. Grinding through that job made me alert to gaps in general. I soon saw them everywhere, between what's said and done, what's done and meant, what's promised and given. Gaps. Often gulfs. Presumed invisible by their owners, if not also invisible to them.

It made me see that we live in two worlds. All the time. One where shit happens and one where we decide what it was. A gap grows when we decide they weren't the same thing, like those cocktails that don't count in calorie-controlled diets because they're only drinks, which, after all, share a category with water. So well-defended was the world of my upbringing that it took until this decade of my life to untangle it from where I live – a real world. And it's in that untangling, largely driven by writing, and by the experiences I've had and the people I've met, that I've come to see why fiction works. The world of our inner legends and biases, and the streets around us that teem with legends of their own, will always be at odds. And not in conceptual ways but in the most existential way, giving hard outcomes. If you're a police officer accustomed to locker-room banter with colleagues, you know well that in the current climate what you sometimes joke about would end your career if used outside. Then you'd see the two worlds fastidiously separated in a court, word by word, traced to intentions even though you feel you meant none. You'd be judged by one world: the one outside the locker room.

Whatever you do I suspect you live in at least two places. This interplay of worlds is what humanity and therefore literature is about. Our extremes live in the gap. The further our experience from what we hold it to be, the wider it gets, all the way to the chasm governments face when they manufacture crises to justify war. You will know people who stand some distance from where they purport to stand, and probably some who stand opposite. I'm not just talking about the Johnsons, nor outright deceit. Every human initiative is accidentally or deliberately influenced like a Chinese whisper, which can't help but diffract results down the line.

I didn't figure out until later that I'd stumbled on the place religions run to after the world doesn't end when they predicted. The place where the brain erases sticky facts, makes dialogue sound purposeful in retrospect, manufactures belief in lies and in the hopeless, makes excuses for spouses who thrash you and children who're bad. Home of the fallacy. Home of deceit. Home of hope, disappointment, expectation, stalking and love. Home of all conspiracies and anti-conspiracies.

And I wasn't alone there, it was swarming.

The crackling gap between conceptual ideal and existential chaos: where violence is dressed as freedom, autocracy as democracy, desire as need, blame as innocence. Where all credit and most business play for profits.

I was intrigued and dismayed. On the one hand it meant the Johnsons were off the hook. Maybe their minds had scribbled a different memo of the day we loaned them the book. Maybe we remembered loaning it when we hadn't. Or some perceived slight by the Johnsons made them candidates for being fingered over the book when the heat for mislaying it fell on one of us. Maybe we last saw the book in their hands and our brains filed its absence with that sighting, or we chose to file it there. This is the gap. It can be used or abused but few people stay out of it. Like a summary court, you go for decisions, not justice. The book has vanished in existential terms. Despite knowing that our accuracy in matching truth to ideas is less than a hundred per cent, we finger the Johnsons. Perhaps a different agenda hijacks the issue on its way through the gap. Then the Johnsons feel slighted when we don't call them for drinks. Their sourness can soon make us candidates for something, then they don't call us for drinks. So we're slighted, and on and on this tennis of bad ideas throws existential ripples all over your life when in fact the book fell behind a cupboard. If you found the damned thing you'd be better off just leaving it there.

All because we fear the unknown. Chaos. We're a creature who fears existing and 'just because' isn't a good enough answer. So we gather all the clues we can and build our own answer, and if there are no clues we build one anyway, what the hell?

Otherwise our fears crawl there and we're fucked.

The gap. On the other hand it's where controllers hide. All the bitter human torsion and force that skulks behind innocent words comes from there. Look at families you know. Where you see a family taking pains not to 'air its dirty laundry in public' you can find an ethos at some distance from the truth, or from what another family at least would consider ideal. A family with hidden controls and unspoken rules. Yet that can be the family whose pride is most unshakeable because it bases it on words and not actions, and the words are all great. It can't be sinister because it's just how we are.

You're probably aware of all this; indulge me because these ideas lit up like a fairground for me. I'd managed to avoid them not because they're obscure but because it wasn't in my interests to acknowledge them, it would've meant puncturing the place I came from. But now, as the gap's mechanisms lit up and were assigned to the hard feelings and lessons of youth, those experiences began to leave a taste in my mouth like bile after bad tequila. Everything changed. Even the so-called battle between good and bad took a kicking; the actual battle must be between real and unreal. Or else we float somewhere on a spectrum of reality, either nearer to or further from admitting to facts and being guided by them. Fear and confidence must have to do with our position, meaning it can fluctuate. Wealth must sway our perception by buffering us from chaos.

None of this is to say I'm any better at it. It all just flew up into a focusing lens, making dumb youth more of a trip to put behind me than I could've imagined. I'd stumbled on the quantum place where yes meant no, where black was white, where losing an election made you president. The more I examined the space between the real and what we construe as real, the more it felt like a backstage pass to the human condition, a key to our central dilemma.

I learned that I was fucking weird. That humans are fucking weird and that we inhabit houses-of-cards made of bent ideas. That anyone with confidence is dangerously deluded; that anyone without it is fucking doomed.

You don't have to hold these positions to be a writer. They fit here because the gap is also where characters in books live their lives. Literature is about people and their truths, which means conflict because our truths are rarely the same. As writers we decide what the reader can know that the character doesn't, we build gaps and arm conflicts. We could always set our stories in moral and evolutionary climates without gaps, but for me the climate we have is wild. It begs attention. The way things are, if you wrote reality verbatim it would be rejected as unnatural, so much do we live in ideas and not facts. If we saw the true intent behind our actions we'd be horrified.

Step back and see what truly goes on. It's a ratfuck.

If you chase these ideas to their conclusion they also define a whole meaning of life. Whether you subscribe to it or not, it's a strong position from which to play God with characters. The next chapter strips us down to those bones.

*Man is the only animal for whom his own existence
is a problem which he has to solve.*

Erich Fromm

2 THE WORLD

Animals on this planet are born knowing what they have to do. They just go out and do it. If you raise an anteater in isolation from other anteaters it will still have a taste for ants, and will go out and find them. But humans aren't born with such programs. We come with an operating system and the blessing or curse of self-consciousness; the rest is up to us. What the human mind does by nature is look for order, and because self-conscious reality is random and terrifying it makes a lot of it up in the form of ideals, schemes and beliefs. Not that we invent a world from scratch – although we also can – but that our world can be a careful selection of wishes and half-truths. A gist of a world, where the unseen is described by ideas. So that, in a way, what separates us from the animals is our ability to bullshit ourselves.

From this position, choosing from the values around us, we each make a pact with Destiny. The mystic makes a pact that he will be saved by an invisible being if he does certain things such as kneel and talk to himself. He might not be saved if he does certain others, such as eat the wrong food. The engineer makes a pact that he can't be saved beyond his scientifically expected lifespan, and that instead his work is to save himself materially using reason. He might also be forsaken if he eats the wrong food, but in his case it's food which science has rejected.

It's not convenient for the mystic to reflect that a random number of people who kneel and talk to themselves still perish in uncomfortable ways, and are never heard from again; nor for the engineer to reflect that science routinely reverses its conclusions. Both characters are firm in their pacts. Both avoid certain foods and follow ideas for which there may be no material evidence.

Then intellect goes to work. It works to attach universality, history and eternity to the chosen ideas. So the mystic not only believes that he will be saved but that everyone will be saved if they follow the same ideas – he makes the pact universal and adds that things have always and will always be that way, and that it's the only way. Moreover, he grows to believe it self-evident. Likewise, the engineer is sure that only science can save. He even defines his salvation differently.

Regardless of how those ideas arose – and these samples harm neither advocate, they can still be correct – both exist only in the mind. Their only application is through the human body, and is the only point at which they touch hard reality. What's more, because we're guided by our concepts in everything we do, we tend to filter out evidence that doesn't support our beliefs. So the mystic sees signs of his creator, the engineer notes the hand of science, the pessimist sees trouble ahead.

Of course we routinely take our biases into account. But what blew my mind was finding that even the world where our biases grow is a construction. And we rarely take *that* into account. Think back to history class at school, the one where the Spaniards did this, the French did that, or an Italian said something five centuries ago. Then recall that until recently there was no Italy. There was no Spain or France. Distinct peoples, often without a common language, have been grouped under a nationalist idea that didn't arise until centuries after they supposedly acted in its history.

Just like childhood – a quite recent idea.

National patriotism – a recent idea.

Ambition as a positive trait – a recent idea.

Fatherly love – a recently returned idea.

The two-sex model of man versus woman – an old idea.

Romantic love between siblings – a vanished idea.

Homosexuality as a variant type – an idea on its way back out.

Each of our accepted ideas overthrows the one before until it passes for an unbroken truth spanning all of time. So today we believe that fathers by nature show love to their offspring, that those offspring by nature enjoy a period of playful childhood, that they belong to a nation greater than themselves which defines their cultural background and sets a social climate on their behalf, that they may pursue romantic relationships with either sex, that such relationships with their siblings would be wrong, and that their ambitions will dictate the extent of their success. Yet until quite recently these things were not only different but reversed. And in many places they still are, which gives on to the broader issue: that there are enough of us across varied-enough territories that our ideas are always different. So we influence others and form societies. In many societies children can marry, but men can't be with men. In others, men can be with men, but children can't marry; and both groups feel certain that their ideas are a culmination of progress and a correction of previously primitive ideas. In this case they're social mores, bound by culture, but the same applies to governing ideologies. For instance, communists are certain of two things: that they've identified the only proper way for humans to govern themselves, and that other ideas are wrong. Capitalists are certain of the same through a completely reverse philosophy, and neither will admit to being part of a nominal experiment. Rather, they attach the certainty of eternity to their ideas, helped by our confinement in the present, where today's idea is the obvious one. This is where it gets interesting for me. In running our respective experiments – ideologies, governments, wars, religions, football matches and individual lives – it falls to our ideas to predict the future. We plot what will happen in existential terms if we follow a particular conceptual course of action, such as prepare for an uprising, a second coming, an economic slump, a climate crisis or the end of the world. Whole generations can throw their lives at predicted outcomes, but see how infrequently they ever happen: rarely in the way we prepare for them, if at all. History shows our success rate to be about the same as tossing dice.

Meanwhile, reality throws up the emergencies that weren't predicted, which keeps our memory of failed predictions short. Whoever made the predictions is safe: time and chaos feed the gap with new stuff to explain miscalculations and to predict with more certainty that the world will end next year. That equation of short memory, shifting time, and chaos is the darling of governments dodging trouble: whenever a scandal erupts they launch official enquiries that put matters beyond discussion until we care less. By the time a verdict is reached, a dozen new crises have passed.

Even so, we keep the faith. Discrepancies between the nominal and the real may disturb us but our tolerance is high. This owes to the same phenomenon that allows literature to work at all: *people more easily believe an idea than a fact.*

Only ideas have order – just what the mind looks for.

It might seem to an alien watching us that human history derives from our constant interference in the gap between prediction and reality. A sharp alien would also see that it constitutes an engine. Our struggle to manifest ideas in reality does cause change, and some success; and either way there's reciprocal action, as we change the environment it changes us – we plough fields, they make us strong, that strength passes in genes to adapt future ploughmen. Which suggests that if as a species we survive the risks of our intermediate ideas we might actually harmonise with chaos one day. The problem is that we don't know what form order might take. It seems increasingly likely that we're light-years away from understanding ourselves and the universe, if there's anything to understand. For the time being our minds seem to strive for order because it feels natural. We feel as if the universe has order. As if only humans are chaotic. So order is our aiming point by nature, as if we were just trying to get home.

According to these ideas we also feed reciprocal action by fucking up and challenging order, probably feed it more than by obedience. There lies our workspace: because as airtight as current ideas might seem – the planet as a single ecosystem, nature as a self-balancing organism, peace as an outcome of freedom – their cracks are already appearing.

That's where we come in.

The most beautiful things are those that madness prompts and reason writes.

André Gide

3 BAD TEQUILA

All these ideas and their ramifications made me want to shout. I shouted on paper. The hitch is that it takes longer to shout a novel than a song, and I'm not a musician. I needed patience to sit through the job, and I found it in another gift from home. It sprang from the fact that you can toss an occasional half-truth through the gap on a whim, but running a long-term ethos at any variance from the truth requires an immune system. It needs it to attack inconvenient facts and convert them into forms it can metabolise and put to its own use. Our enemies have one: *again they fail and we gloriously triumph*. We have one: *again they fail and we gloriously triumph*. And my household had one: *the fucking Johnsons kept that book*.

To keep a household regulated, an immune system patrols all the values that enter its environment of ideas. In practical terms it means constantly monitoring, prying, testing and reinforcing the status quo, loading half of all conversation with whiskers and traps. It means every time you say 'Johnson' you hear 'book' until you don't bring it up any more. The Johnsons kept the book, you are the black sheep, I am the innocent martyr and your father is the silent hero. If these are the positions in a household script, the immune system will patrol even the farthest perimeter, generations of ideas away, to herd things back to that order. You can find the damned book behind a cupboard and somehow it's still the John-sons' fault, or someone's fault. But then you liked the Johnsons, didn't you? And you're a black sheep, so they must be black sheep, so you all flock together. Bang – you're implicated by association, without recourse to justice because underneath the mesh of ideas against you stands one existential lever: the book, which was missing. The point is that it was all too much shit for me as a child. I distrusted it. Cross-referencing all the values wires you into a steel cocoon.

Its weight along with the immune system's intrusive-ness made me a loner from a young age. Rather than leave independent ideas at the door I learned to pay lip-service to the system's expectations then go to a corner and reflect by myself. It gave me a taste for solitude and set me up to write the distance of a novel. It fostered habits of observation and reflection, because whatever position you hold in a group, in however subtle a way, its spider's web of values can be reverse-engineered to a true meaning. And those meanings interested me, as disappointing as they often were. I sensed that life's actual script, the one that directs intent, was written there.

So the gifts of these headfucks met two requirements of writing: something to say and the patience to say it. All it needed was a spark.

It came when I saw our culture's ethos grow into the one I left behind.

And saw that it wanted to monitor, distort and re-inforce its ideas in exactly the same way.

And I know how that goes.
That taste of shit tequila is why I write.

At least according to this seamless conceptual model.

The existential thread is simpler: I was unemployed, frustrated. These ideas ignited one day over a news clip of an American kid being arrested.
I wrote a page in anger and liked it.

And the only Johnsons I ever knew were great people.
I would've gift-wrapped the book.

Anyway.

Let's write one.

Some people never go crazy. What truly horrible lives they must lead.

Charles Bukowski

4 CRAZY

I think you'll know if you have an ability. I think you'll feel it. Over time you couldn't miss certain powers on the move inside. Inklings. I may be wrong but I think it's true. The problem is that over the past century of self, at least in our sheltered workshop of the world, we've all been told how uniquely special we are, sending our powers of self-judgement to fuck; on top of that, the standards by which ability is judged have been lowered across the culture, to avoid anyone suffering the stress of unspecialness. So we're a milieu that holds itself full of ability, and we need to take that into account.

This chapter arises because if we propose to write then we sense we're about to throw ourselves into an abyss which could really destroy our illusions. We're about to test that inkling, which if it's a good inkling will have become a banker in life. And surely the key to a good and productive life is to not test your inklings but leave them alone, use their quiet warmth to generate confidence in lesser things. Because writing a book, especially a literary one, isn't like basketball. If you fail at basketball, you fail at basketball. If you fail at literature you risk failing as a person, because your full matrix of being is at work in it. So this is the bit where I warn DON'T DO IT! *Are you fucking crazy?* The odds of finishing a book are thousands to one!

That's the warning out of the way. If you're like me, you'll ignore it. If like me you have self-defeating demons, you'll say, 'Fuck them.' Anyway, if we fail we can always do the human thing and blame something else. The Johnsons. Or conditions were wrong. When did we ever take the full blame on our backs?

So to the central issue: deciding if we're the ones who should do this, or if we're out of our minds. I can't say, you'll have to decide – but these ideas can make a cradle for argument. Because some of us, held above our station by the likes of doting family, can be convinced we have an ability when we haven't. We're the ones whose delusions people watch survive death at talent-show auditions. They marvel that nobody around us ever said, 'You cannot fucking sing.' They wonder what psychological house of mirrors we've been stuck in to be so starved of accurate feedback. Though now: I don't believe you need a gift to write, it can also be done with a medical technician's skill, the methods are outlined in Part Three. Here let's explore the one risk that nips at the heels of every untested writer – the risk of catastrophic failure.

I shared a house with surfers who were also chefs in their last year of college. I'd eaten in impressive restaurants before but the surfing chefs were a whole new blast, alchemists with the solemn fervour of illegal surgeons. I was inspired. They used herbs and seeds and oils I'd never heard of, knives so rare that washing-up could destroy them, and a creole kitchen language fit for pirates.

I hadn't cooked much before then, but after watching them I knew that I could. They'd see random things in the fridge and turn them into art, anything at all. They were food conjurers. Surely I could do that. Why not? The keys were passion, imagination. So they made a fanfare when I said I'd cook for them one night, cook for everyone in the house and their dog. When the night came they sat around the table toasting me in anticipation. I went to work like a Frenchman, alert and frowning. Finally, after some frenzied boiling, a chef came over to look in the pot. There was a creeping silence. What I'd made was fusilli pasta with salt, yoghurt and grapes. Then, finding it not quite up to my mind's palate, I added vinegar. So on top of it being shit it also curdled. I may have tried to cover that with parsley. All this sank in against the sound of someone phoning for pizza.

Now: I don't think I had a bad palate back then. I'd eaten food all over the world, observed and enjoyed its preparation. And I can more or less cook today, if nothing like the surfing chefs. I must've had the basics in me at least, even then. So what the fuck? Obviously I've done worse shit in my life, it's an anecdote, a laugh. But I mention it for being a moment of confidence in some creation, with all the right tools and conditions in place. Some people cook badly, pair the wrong ingredients, get too ambitious – but this was in another league, this was 'What the fuck are you really trying to do? Vinegar and grapes?'

More recently I took part in a book show with some writers overseas. After the readings everyone mingled and had a drink. A well-dressed young woman who had been in the audience came up to me with some papers and a business card, and said that I should consider doing another event, actually a cycle of ground-breaking events that she was planning. It's usual at these events to be approached by other organisers – literary shows are flowerbeds in the pollination cycle. This young woman spoke perfect English and was clearly of an educated class – but something wasn't right, my bullshit alarm rang earlier than usual. For one thing, she regaled me like a long-lost friend, all about her life-changing achievements. It soon became clear that she was talking crap. Not drug- or alcohol-induced crap but plausible-sounding gibberish, strings of pseudo-sentences made up of quotes and dogma, sentences with a semblance of meaning, with all the right sounds, the right rapport-building gestures – but unconnected, without reference to my replies, without meaning.

I accepted her calling card and papers. Under her name on the calling card, running off the bottom and across the back, it read:

There is no way but then why are we here! STOP THE ABUSE! Mandela and the world to keep living organisation as one THE WORLD CONVOCATORIUM OF FREEDOM listen to his words and say WHY! All good things must come to an end TECHNICAL DIRECTOR OF PEACE AND FREEDOM call today or it could be too late EXCELLENCE do it! Events and planning requirements global and universal professionalism EXTREME ACHIEVEMENT!

Something caught my eye behind her. It was the host waving at me to give her the slip. I passed her on to another group of drinkers and joined the organisers. According to them the woman's shtick was as a literary icon and essential face on the arts scene. They said she'd already once been removed from a show for being a pest. Glancing over her papers I saw they were a badly photocopied extension of the card, a William Burroughs cut-up of liberal parlour dogma – but cut up as if by a lawnmower.

It only took ten minutes to meet her and live this anecdote but there's something sobering in it, and it's this: she thought she was being great. She dressed herself immaculately, got herself across town, used first-class language and syntax to express a passionate personal calling – and it was bollocks.

I say it here because it reminds me of yoghurt and grape pasta. What book would I have written that day? What would my calling card have said? Now: I have a sense this girl was more permanently off-track, it's a banker in my life to think she was. But who knows. She didn't write a book that day, I didn't write a book on my day. But I wrote one later, which to me says: there's crazy and there's *fucking crazy*. There's weird and there's *fucking weird*. Neuroses and conflict are fine backgrounds and fuels for writing about life, if we survive them they not only give us something to write about but often the delusional optimism to write it. But we still have to put the words down, and in the right order. It's not as easy as thinking them. We've both listened in wonder to people mouthing off like machine guns, about having hatched from an egg, a set of matching heroes, envy on Mars.

But it's not workable writing until it's written down and makes some fucking sense.

So then crazy is good – having been crazy, sporadically crazy, latently crazy, potentially crazy – but if you're *actually* crazy it might be impossible to write a book, at least one with meaning and rapport. A constant effort in one direction is called for. If you're an experimental writer then go for it. Otherwise the question of how accurately we perceive our abilities, or if we're really bananas, is a central question, because the job also needs the focus and persistence of a good carpenter, and it needs self-honesty, it needs judgement. If I had to pick a modern condition to write from I'd pick OCD over dependence, mania over depression, anxiety over histrionics. For those of us with flashes of everything, which is to say average contemporary western beings, I say the maths governing our chances of attracting ridicule are the same as those governing the number of idiots on the road: I consider myself a good driver but I still make an error in traffic once in a while. If you take it as an average and then add a thousand drivers on the road, the deluge of idiots is explained. Likewise, human fluctuations can drive us out of basic character and make us absurd to those who witness those spikes, but it doesn't make us crazy all the time. We can even spike frequently, it doesn't disqualify us from later writing a book because a book takes time, we'd have to be absurd across all that time to wholly fail. The beauty of writing is that we can go over it again and again. It can suckle from shifting moods and still enjoy the smoothing of time.

This suggests a curve governing personalities and writing where foibles and demons are a benefit to the job, both an irritant and a tool for understanding and forgiving humanity – but only up to a point. Crazy is good, fucking crazy is bad. Crazy can be used, fucking crazy is useless. Once we can certify to ourselves that we're merely crazy or merely weird, we then move on to the main psychological challenge: fear of not measuring up. And if you have that, join the club.

My money is on the writer who has it and conquers it, not the one who starts confident and stays confident. I lost my confidence after adding vinegar to the pot, the girl with the calling card stayed confident; but she was confident in the face of all evidence. Confidence was all she had. I don't suggest it's a human trait, nor mine or yours specifically, to wander around fearing failure – but it's one that attaches particularly to writing. Understandably: to write an honest book we have to reveal strands of ourselves that we may not have even acknowledged. The pool we splash in to write is one of psychology and spirit, and the only rock we can cling to is the truth. It offers no shade or shelter but still we have to cling there or drown. An amazing thing then happens, which is at the heart of our need to read and write: once we dive under a storyline we find truths, things that we aren't alone in. Things that nobody else has acknowledged either. Then we're really talking. Then we're really writing. We don't connect to the grandfather figure till we see him naked and frail in his bath. And the fear that applies there is that such truths are invasive and inappropriate. If the scene is modelled on our own grandfather we'll face resistance in writing him completely. I heard of an exercise used in a writing workshop that involved imagining a photograph so personal that we couldn't show it to anyone. What would it be? That's the level of exposure we're aiming for. All based on the notion that literature exists to speculate on things we can't talk about in the street. Who cares what Emma looks for in a partner, we want to know her darkest secret.

Once we slay the main fear – traditionally dressed as procrastination – other pitfalls show up that we need to keep an eye on. They stem from this: there are two ways around the fear of being crap – one is by not being crap, the other is by convincing ourselves that we're not, and the latter is easiest to do when we're feeling good about our writing. But feeling good can come from three places: writing well and knowing it; being spontaneous; or writing about something so personally resonant that it stirs our feelings even when badly written. We should only respond to the first of these. Anyone with a background in the arts will know how easy it is to be swept away to creative la-la land. Advertising creatives go there all the time, especially when the pitch is tomorrow morning and they still haven't had the big idea. La-la land is forgivable but over time we have to be able to discern it from the real thing. As a general rule, if you sit down to write in a bubbly mood, la-la land is often where you'll go. Sit down in the calm following difficulty and you're more likely to write weightily. La-la land also leads to what Strunk & White in their classic writing handbook *The Elements of*

Style called 'good old spontaneous me' (wa-hey, so here we go screaming to another oh-so-outrageous tale!), which is a form best left to the lower echelon of media celebrities. You'll generally recognise good old spontaneous writing if you lay it down and look again another day; it's the crap that makes you wince.

The third case – writing from strong personal feelings – is probably the trickiest because big feelings survive any length of laying down. It's the case that needs us to be most objective and soul-searching. It probably accounts for most manuscripts by would-be mothers about their childlessness, singles about their last partner's treachery, victims of illness about their valiant struggle. There's no argument that these books should be written, but maybe their writing is the end in itself, a valid cry but only for the person with those feelings. Those books presuppose that we will have the same strong feelings by default, and thus plotting, form and style can be set aside.

Case in point, a man approached me once with a manuscript. He felt it could be the Next Big Thing if it had the right agent. It featured a toddler he'd left after a failed relationship. The book's opening had him arriving home in happier times, which meant verbatim dialogue between 'Mommeeeee' and 'Daddeeeeee' and 'Widdle babieeeeeee'. It was as heartbreaking to read as the man's relationship must have been to live, but in a bad way. And the man wasn't crazy. He loved books, was well read – but his writing in this case played thunderous notes on an inner piano that the rest of us just don't have. It's not to say the story couldn't be beautifully told, that it couldn't give us those feelings – but it would have to build that piano first. It means the energy from our feelings can't always be spat directly onto a page, except to write a letter we never send. That energy instead has to propel us through the journey of writing as well as we can. It means we have to be able to stand back and see our theme in all its dimensions. It means the book about the psycho lover also shows his good qualities and isn't a straight assassination. Before starting to write we need to assure ourselves that we're not out to settle a score (or if we are, to make sure we do it symbolically or indirectly and with craft), and that we're not stuck in a feeling-land where little Archie's first birthday party would feel just as amazing to everyone else as it did to us. Nobody is interested in little Archie unless something big happens at the party.

If we can certify that our viewpoint, as weird or crazy as it might be, is also seen by us as weird and crazy, then it can be made an asset of, and all we have to worry about is the fear. We first have to admit that some of us are ridiculous; or as I do, admit to being ridiculous some of the time. It might also be helpful here, as we're tooling up to become writers, to shift our thinking from the notion that we are or should be single coherent selves. It's another long-held idea, a theory that's reflected in all our talk of 'finding ourselves', 'defining ourselves', 'being true to ourselves' – that somehow everything we do comes from a single place. Surely, within the cogs of inner and outer existence we are different some of the time. A father manifests differently than a son, a friend differently than an enemy. And we can be absurd some of the time.

The point to take is that as writers we can be weird and crazy and awkward and wrong – but there also has to be something else. Our efforts can rock, pitch and slide, but we have to know roughly what centre feels like, and what forward motion is. Centre is the place from where we witness ourselves and monitor our thoughts. For the purposes of writing, our thoughts are not our selves – the voice watching our thoughts is our self. That place is the one reading this. It has to take the generated heat of our madness, frustration, anger and dismay, and distil it into one gaseous mass. We can do it by just thinking of it that way. That mass is rocket fuel. Every strong feeling is rocket fuel, a clean multipurpose fuel, not to be spat raw onto a page but to drive us to sit there and scheme and craft and confess. If the neighbour pisses you off – rocket fuel. If your lover leaves you – rocket fuel. If your old man presses those buttons again – fucking rocket fuel. Collect it and think of yourself collecting it. Realise it. Make it a philosophy. Every night before you sleep imagine yourself gathering it and focusing it in writing. Use your compulsions – anger, excess, melancholy, hyperactivity; use that HANGOVER, use the tail of an explosive day – harness those forces, become single-minded, learn to admit to yourself the state of animus you're in and say, 'This is rocket fuel.' Rocket fuel, rocket fuel, rocket fuel. And in those gales of feelings mysterious things will happen which are beyond arrangements of words – then it can be art. Compose later, edit later, assess it another day – just get it down. At the risk of sounding like *The Secret*, the mind is a puppy, we can train it to do remarkable things.

I can't make mine turn me into a paragon of productivity and virtue, I'd be frightened if I were the type to try. But, from experience, this kind of visualisation can work in specific bursts, and writing is that way. Anyway, we're not looking for a fucking miracle, we don't have to grow big teeth and move to Malibu, we don't have to lift a car off a baby; we just have to stick at writing. We just have to grind through it. If you're coming to it from a darker place, also imagine yourself every night gathering all the piles of shit everyone has ever put on you into a single mammoth pile – and over the course of a few weeks watch extraordinary fronds and, eventually, plants, trees and flowers sprout from it.

Then in that hour of night when you're ready to quit, say 'rocket fuel', summon it, or pick a rare flower. I believe that anyone can write more or less, but good writing takes a little bit more – and great writing only happens in the extra mile, after others have given up. Rocket fuel might get us there.

I heard an author say that there are two kinds of writers: channellers and plodders. The channeller believes in inspiration and feels like an instrument of unseen forces, the plodder puts one word after another and builds his work brick by rational brick. I'll propose that we can use both approaches in separate seasons, we'll get to them later. For now think about the variety of writers out there in the dark, because we'll become one of them and we should make the decision of which to become. There are writers who have yet to write a word who will go on to write masterpieces. There are writers who have yet to write a word and never will, but who could have gone on to write masterpieces. There are writers who have begun one of the classics of our time who will be conquered by fear and never finish it. There are some who will finish the book fifteen years after it was relevant. There are some who will write acceptable books but no more. There are some who will burn with the certainty that writing is their calling and then write twelve volumes of crap. There are some who are railway lovers whose detailed love of railways will delight railway lovers everywhere. There are some clever people who will write a good book and find that it's enough.

Then there's you, and there's me.

Any fear we have is just an idea, and if that's our main challenge, then fuck it. As to why we should write at all: if we're both here looking at this, that thirst must spring from somewhere. Writing is what it is, every word is visible for everyone to see, and it is when it is, whenever we make that be. The ancient Greeks had a word which for me expresses it perfectly: *kairos* – the right moment. Something beyond coincidence or luck, the idea that we can't know the extent to which any action we take is driven by internal complexes, even ancestral complexes handed down to us. Although we end up thinking everything we do is the result of rational choice-making, when we add to life's algorithm the external forces that guide us to action, widespread cultural movements and actions by which we might be swept up, internal forces and complexes, the amount of current external conditions that are the result of previous choices, and the unforeseen future effects of the choices we make today, we end up stuffing it into the concept of Fate. But once we figure out that these threads make it up, we can no longer access its innocence, and luck isn't a detailed enough idea to express it any more.

So for us about to write, here asking whether we should or shouldn't, now conscious of all the maths swirling around us, but also about to ignore it; for us who are merely crazy and prepared to cock a snook at fear, all the threads behind us that bring us to this page, and all those that will follow from here; everything we are in the face of them, and all that we might be – are in *kairos*.

The right moment.

This one may as well be it.

Books should be built of one's tissue or not at all.

Lawrence Durrell

5 STORIES

To start the engine, pick any story. I'll pick one: there was a friend in my class called Charlie. His grandmother had a macaw parrot. I loved parrots, and especially macaw parrots. It seemed uncanny to know somebody who had one, macaws were almost as big as me, they were zoo parrots, movie parrots. Charlie's grandma had one. I used to ask after her health, then after the parrot's.

One day Charlie said that his grandmother couldn't deal with the parrot any more. It was noisy and made a mess, and she was getting old. He knew I already had a menagerie at home, and asked if I would take it.

'Hell, yeah,' I said. I spent some days dreaming about the parrot's arrival, then Charlie came around with the bird on a perch. It was a magnificent bird, a scarlet macaw, red, yellow, green and royal blue. 'Does it have a cage?' I asked.

'No, it lives on the perch.'

'Won't it fly away?'

'Its wings are clipped.'

So I left the parrot on its perch and within a day saw the fucker circling overhead at two hundred feet. It wasn't a great flier – but it could fly. It did a victory lap and flew away. I ran onto the street and saw it land high up in a tree two houses away on the corner. I didn't know who lived in that house, but it was the corner I caught the school bus from, and the gardener there was called Rufino. He was a good man and soon went up the tree to grab the bird, even though he was portly.

But when he got close the bird flew away

So with the parrot gone, the point is this: I've picked a random anecdote from childhood and told it as I would in speech, more or less a bare story – but by now an engine runs in it. It can go places. Hopefully apart from concern for the bird, you feel some sympathy for Charlie, and some for me. The anecdote has framed two equal friends and armed a problem between them. Each has a viewpoint: to Charlie, the bird is a cherished family mascot of many years which I have neglected and lost within a day. To me, Charlie has conveniently removed one of his grandmother's problems to my house and neglected any measures to keep it put. Conflict. Now we want to know where it will end. Where can it go? The case is that we're involved in the story. It has everything we need for writing: imagine it was the first scene in a novel where Charlie and I were later pitched against each other as adults vying for the same prize. We would know the scene was significant in some way, and would wait to see how. Would it mean that Charlie held a grudge that authorised underhandedness? Or would I capitulate owing to feelings of guilt? The answers would lie in whatever transpired between Charlie and I after I told him about the bird's disappearance; but if we left that part out, wouldn't it create tension throughout the book, wondering how that scene would affect the outcome? Obviously Charlie's a great guy, our friendship would appear to continue – but underneath that, in the dark where novels take place, we would know the scene held clues to the outcome. If we wanted to really string out the tension we could release the anecdote scene by scene, until just before the climax when we're pitted against each other – and then the parrot flies away. Anything can happen in our story: if it's a TV movie the parrot eventually returns and everyone lives happily ever after, if it's literature the parrot gets run over and both characters undergo life-changing crises, if it's fantasy the parrot liberates all the parrots in the jungle.

In having written down a story, any story where something happens, we have the opening to something much bigger. And a beautiful mystery of the writing process is that whatever that first story is, you will end up writing what you have to write as a result of it. Maybe not a parrot, but raise the stakes with the same elements: Charlie and I are in a crime gang, and when Charlie goes to prison for a year he entrusts his beautiful wife to me to watch over. He brings her around to my house, but after one night she disappears on a binge and I have to find her before Charlie gets out. Better still, she has the chequebook Charlie needs to survive in jail. Until I find her I have to pay for Charlie, but after a month I'm so broke I resort to gambling, and before long I'm being chased by debt-collectors; then on my last outrageous gamble, with everything riding on a win – I meet Charlie's wife. Maybe she's who I have to play. Maybe we fall in love and run off.

Maybe she's who put Charlie in jail.

It all started with the parrot on paper. It doesn't matter how insignificant our stories are, they're telling because we want to tell them. Writing of something you've done yourself is all you need to add life to a book, and that breath can fly into new stories. If what brings you to these pages is a deep and specific emotional issue, don't start with that, first write a little story and look at it. Whatever burns inside you will start building what you have to write in parallel to any story, at a safe distance, and the engine in your writing will start running on its own. It's a feature of monkeys that you can't approach them face-on, you have to come from the side and look at them sideways; and writing is that way, especially if you come to it with strong feelings. By setting up a parallel track with characters other than yourself, the story can draw from your feelings without self-consciousness. It frees you to write a great book.

Simple stories and simple writing are beautiful, but also bear in mind that in modern writing there's a reductive effect to take account of. It means if I'd merely lost the parrot for an hour, all the same elements would be there but it would be too small an event to excite us. Action has to be large in our stories, nobody's interested in people with vague drives overcoming moderate opposition. Remember the feelings of your first date, first love, first break-up. That shit was life or death.

Now's the time to ask: what shall we write? Where can we go? You might know already, or you might not, but if we're going with the modern flow we should write about conflict – and it's not as simple as throwing enemies onto a page. Start small, let the thing grow. And don't give the punchline away too early, which brings me back to the duty of Charlie's grandmother's parrot. I scoured the area for it, put the word out on the streets. But the bird had vanished. We never saw it again.

'You must have tortured it,' Charlie growled the next day. 'You must have beaten it and tried to have sex with it and tortured it with instruments!'

He growled it every day for the rest of my school life.

Smiling.

Writing is a socially acceptable form of schizophrenia.

E. L. Doctorow

6 LICENCE

A man came up to me at a reading. The show was in a fine old pub. He said he liked my work and wanted to be a writer himself. He said he'd decided to follow my example and set himself up in the right way for writing. I listened with interest for what the right way might be. I wondered what in my writing or person even suggested there was a right way, and from which parts of either he'd taken it.

The man joined me behind the venue for a smoke and said he'd chosen that week to begin his new life as a writer. 'I'm just going for it,' he said. 'This is it.' Then he handed me a pendant and said it was a gift. On the pendant was written a Bukowski quote: 'The tigers have found me, and I do not care.'

I got it. It didn't explain how I'd become a poster boy for it, but what he meant to achieve was a sense of licence. I believe in that, big-time. We can go timidly into some things but not into writing. The pendant said it all. We have to bury ourselves and dig our way out. Nobody else can license us, we have to license ourselves, we have to make a pact for the abyss and not give a shit. Write or die. There might be a reason why so many of the greatest figures in literature were fucking messes, or the reason might be why so many fucking messes became great figures in literature. But aside from madness, aside from the detriments they brought to the game, which didn't even necessarily help, they all had a licence. They authorised themselves to throw everything at writing, to throw their lives away into it. To live badly, eat poorly, be impossible – not that we calculate these things but that we license ourselves to be oblivious to them, to tolerate them, to even enjoy the energy that flies off a rub of self-destruction. I write again as though the only real writers are maniacs, and I apologise, it's not true, there are many balanced writers, even a whole school of thought that says we should live as humdrum a life as possible to better focus our adventures on the page – but by madness I mean any level of conflict or foible, down to the ones that writing itself provokes. From where I sit, deciding to live a humdrum life is a strong reaction, and mad in itself. And again there might be something of the fleeing effect: madness makes us write, writing drives us mad. The thing is that as surely as firemen don't survive their jobs without fireproof gear, we need gear too and it's in our minds. It doesn't matter so much if we're out to write a commercial thriller, although it still can – but if we're coming to the page with feelings, if we're writing from ourselves, it can start a blaze. And if we have a kill-switch – psychological programming to fail or come second – it will physically obstruct us when we begin to write well, or to write of our own dark.

Then fireproof gear is the least of it.

In history an artist's licence to grow strange was recognised in many places. I think it still holds today in the minds of many people, although individualism and cultural neurosis make it easier to fit in with the crowd. I don't suggest that we pretend to grow mad in order to write, but that writing is not necessarily comfortable and its effects will change us in ways that other jobs won't. It may also attract those already closer to an edge. I believe in the artist's licence to be weird, solitary, outrageous, be whoever it takes to make the work happen. You can walk the street in pyjamas if you're an artist, have a pet hyena, sleep under a bridge. All provided you're in the process of outputting art. It's not the cappuccino licence, where you just go without shaving, wear stupid glasses or throw tantrums – I mean really doing it, for better or worse.

If you feel you're totally balanced, you might foster a sense of licence by pacing around in a torn dressing-gown, cursing. The state we're trying to achieve is one of having nothing to lose. Having nothing to lose is a powerful position – the most powerful. If you're coming to this from the balanced middle classes, however, without secrets, compulsions or madness – *if that's fucking possible* – you'll need to see Part Three and become a diligent technician. Technique is a clean mental job that can make any story a page-turner, and it can be done wearing a suit. Otherwise, for nothing to lose, join the rest of us. Thomas Wolfe had to get naked and fondle his balls in order to write. The thing is: we don't care any more. We're writing now. It's a serious job. The stakes are all or nothing. And we have nothing to lose. Everything within our control is now subservient to the writing.

The reason to make a big deal out of licence is this: we have to dismantle the censors in our heads. There's a sense in which that means dismantling our selves. A bank clerk doesn't have to do it, nobody really has to but us. One reason we're held back in writing is the restraints which have been installed as part of our civilisation and preparation for conformity. Conformity is a powerful drive, that shit is old and deep. I believe everyone carries a jury in their mind, of their parents, their heroes, their friends. Of society. To understand its hidden tendrils, take a sample of twenty people you deal with professionally. Five of them will think another five are dicks. Doing the maths, it means we will be dicks to at least that many. None of them have called us one, and we haven't called any of them one, nor passed on the news that one thinks another is one. But we guess where everyone stands. We now have a mental jury installed to run that value algorithm. It's that jury which decides what we can and can't do, and when we've gone too far. When I set out to write *Vernon God Little* I fell into the trap at once, without even thinking. Having found some value in the first pages I started thinking of the work as something worthwhile, with a value. And by two chapters later I didn't like it any more. It was suddenly self-conscious and wooden. I was forced to sit back and uncover what had happened between the first pages, written in an almost unconscious fit, and these pages that wanted to explain and justify themselves. Justify themselves to whom? That was the question – who was I now writing for? Who could be such a stranger in my head that I was self-conscious around them? It was the jury, now with a couple of characters who were photofit impressions of what readers would be like. I couldn't believe it. Even more terrifying: next to them I found my parents on the jury. What was happening on this fucking jury was suddenly a crime of psychology, a mayhem. My parents were there with fantasy readers, then a couple of the most abandoned nutcases I ever called friends. And I understood: the writing had my friends' abandoned seal of approval, then was being buried and justified at every turn for the parents, and polished like old wood for the readers. The exercise was like watching myself lie to my folks about how their car ended up in the pool.

It wasn't too difficult to identify the actual jury – try it. Some members change according to the situation, which I went on to think must be an answer to conspiracy theories – as in, yes, there is a conspiracy, but the actors change. So with the jury. I ended up thinking it was a cultural duty to eliminate it. It's the same thing that kicks in when a reporter shoves a microphone into your face and you suddenly say what everyone else would say. They ask you about cocaine and you say, 'What a problematic issue,' instead of the truth that the capital fucking runs on it. You start saying what we hear on every report, the shit we expect to hear; and you discover that we expect to hear it because that's all we ever say into microphones. An example of the two worlds we live in, all because we installed this jury to save us from being embarrassed or arrested; a little set of spokespeople to remind us what's not expected of a joke.

For our job we must kill it. SACK THE JURY. Check who's on it and eliminate them for the purpose of writing.

Write as if nobody will ever see the work, make a pact never to reveal it. We have to write as if even we're not in the room.

Granted, it can take more than a torn dressing-gown.

This is a shortcut. This little detour usually begins a couple of chapters into your first book, when you analyse your unhappiness with what you're writing and discover that it comes from not knowing who the reader is, which makes you unable to decide how far to go. If in your daily life you like to please people, the effect can be pronounced. Who is the fucking reader? Then if you're unlucky you'll unwittingly discover that a lot of how-to-write books are written not by writers but by editors who go on to say that you should define your genre and market. The old chestnut is: 'If you tell us your story is so original that it resembles nothing else, we will not know what shelf to sell it from.'

Fuck that. Nothing will drive you away from your nature faster than trying to imagine what anyone else wants – least of all what the market wants. The market behaves like a school of spooked sardines, jittering flashes in the form of publishers following publishers, agents following agents following publishers following publishers; and all in the opposite business to yours, the business of second-guessing. Leave them to it. If the school swirls behind you one day it will be full of breathy voices saying they always knew you were the next big thing. But they don't know. The only way to write is to put your best foot forward, conquer your fears and write what works for you, what excites you. So, to the above question, there is no reader. There's only you. Write for yourself, as if you'd never show it to a soul. And if you're like me, don't show it to a soul until it excites you across its whole length. Or, a scheme that works for some: write to one nominal person who gets what you're doing. Write to Faulkner.

Make some time of day, some place, some ritual a bridge to your working space. Every time you shut the door to your room, the jury stays outside. Then see what wants to be written. If your hard-wrought scene about the spy seems wooden, let a bigger spy come in and bugger him till you cry with laughter. Be free. If you like your last chapter more than your first, put it first and see what happens. And beware of our romance with what we do. Preciousness is a creeping enemy too. After hours or weeks at a page it can easily happen that every turn of phrase takes on significance for a writer. It needs a judgement call, or the cold light of a few days later, because even with critical faculties we might judge our work fantastic when it's shit. As a key I feel that better writers more often feel their work is crap, but know when they're onto something. That something is signalled through a quickening pulse, not pride at every word's arrangement but bloodlust from the energy on the page, from persecuting an idea before it evaporates. And I say you'll know when it happens.

Written words in any number are hardy things. They can and should be tousled, roughed up and killed. When you have thousands of words before you, your hands are in a visceral mass and you have licence to do anything you want, including destroying them all and never writing again. If you engage with your writing this way, you'll be glued to a mirror: when the writing's crap, you'll feel personally crap, when it's great, you'll feel great. Don't underestimate the syndrome's power. The only real luck of the draw for us (as in it may rely on personality traits outside our control and be as good as an outside factor) is whether we can tell what's crap or not. If you sit in front of your writing from scratch and find it consistently great, you're probably wrong. And it might be worse crap than those who are struggling with crap. But then, self-esteem can be a fluctuating thing, nothing will teach you how it works more than writing. Learn to use other boosts to propel your writing, and learn when crap might not be as bad as you think. If we can grow the balls to look critically at our work and still let ourselves fly on any whim of inspiration; if we're prepared to face eternity – or as Hemingway said, the lack of it – every day; then we can say we're writing.

Then we're writers.

The process leads to the longer payoff, one that a whole sub-genre of self-help manuals must devote itself to – finding ourselves. I don't personally bask in a glow from it, a lot of self-discovery sucks. But you're going to get it if you write honestly, whether you like it or not, and, anyway, it's upheld as life's journey, so suck it up. Suck it up and write it out.

A comprehensive report was published a few years ago on human reactions to imminent death. The report collated decades of air-crash investigation with data from the final minutes of the Twin Towers tragedy in New York.

And the upshot was that when the shit seriously hits the fan, 85 per cent of people will do nothing. Five per cent will become hysterical, and only 10 per cent will act to save themselves. Why? The rest are waiting for someone to tell them what to do. To take charge of them. The writer can't be that way. We have to fall into the 10 per cent, and that's how we justify our licence. We can be obedient and die; or we can survive.

You'll be starting to see how these festering questions can leave you pacing around in bad robes. Locking yourself away in a crucible of secret frustration is where writing comes from. All those tiny defeats and conquests, numbering almost as many as the words in a book, have a cumulative effect on your calm, your moods, your presence in reality. Things get weird with your friends. And speaking of them, and your milieu in general, you'll find that this is a job nobody can help you with. You'll find that, of necessity, it becomes a secret job, a place you must travel to for work where nobody else has been or can ever go. No amount of explanation can bring anyone else on board. You may start by taking comfort from sympathetic noises and encouragement, but you'll notice after a time that it bears no relation to the journey you're really on. In the end you may wish you hadn't told anyone you were writing, because after months or years all their concern will condense into the one most pointless question any writer can be asked: 'How's the book going?' In saying it they ask for a lie or a platitude. It's as pointless as asking 'Are you happy?' in a life of half a billion minutes. The main function of telling anyone that you're going to write a book is to lay irritants for yourself down the track. They can be useful a few months into the job when you're thinking of quitting, because facing the thirty people you've told will be as hard as facing yourself. But be judicious in choosing who to tell, if anyone, unless you're a quitter by nature. If you roam the urban classes be realistic and remember that some of who you tell will wish against your success, and their asking can later become a knife.

In the end there's a simple equation, one that seems borne out by a catalogue of writers and what they wrote: if you come to writing wanting to escape a reality, if things are shitty where you are, if you want to create a different world where someone wins once in a while – you're coming to the right place, as proven by many of the coolest books ever written. License yourself to do it completely.

Putting words in the right order is a different task to managing the passion and licence to do it. Managing it means neither giving up nor dying.

As to the man at the reading in the pub, he told me he'd quit his job that week in readiness to grow poor and write.

'And then,' he said, 'I went to the dog pound and found myself a dog.'

'What kind of dog?' I wondered how it could help.

'The meanest one-eyed fucker they had.'

The tigers have found us, and we do not care.

Writing is easy: all you do is sit staring at a blank sheet of paper until drops of blood form on your forehead.

Gene Fowler

7 PUNCH

I spent late childhood and adolescence practising martial arts. I'd already been boxing for a while when kung fu and the martial arts grew popular again. Karate, taekwondo, hapkido and all the Shaolin stuff. I wished I was Asian. Before that, for some reason I had wanted to be Libyan, so it was a change. I didn't withstand a second of the new rage. Bruce Lee and Chuck Norris didn't need a boxing ring to practise their art, they could do it in a sawmill full of oily wrongdoers, they could go into the middle of a kung fu temple and take on everyone including the master. It was the new cowboys and Indians, the new cops and robbers, and the language was clear: if you're evil you're oily and not as good at kung fu. They didn't need gloves, or even shoes. Plus, under all the kicking, it was more than just sport, it was a doctrine for life.

When the old Chinaman on TV said to Kwai Chang Caine, 'Quickly as you can, snatch this pebble from my hand,' you wondered if you would be fast enough, if you would be ready to go out of the temple and into the world. Existentially it all meant going to sweat in a white cotton suit and kick and yell with other kickers and yellers. We learned to meditate, we learned some self-control, and we learned a ballet that would deck four attackers at once if they stood still and waited their turn. I can still smell the dust and sweat. I can feel the heavy sleep of tendons and bruises. Though I never since bumped into four attackers who would wait their turn, and don't recall having done a class where they all came at once, the phase was important. Among the ideas I took away was one I resorted to for writing. It's a measure of how lost I was that I had to scour every corner of life for ideas that could be useful.

When you're a kid the first thing you want martial arts to help with is breaking shit. You want your hands and feet to carve through solid objects. You want to set up planks and bricks and bust them in two with karate chops. So I was heartened when, among the first lessons, the master said there was a simple technique behind all blows in the martial arts, and it was the one behind the breaking of objects: *don't aim for the target, aim beyond it*. Because, he said, if you aim for the surface your fist will stop there. If you aim behind, it will keep travelling through. And it's true.

When I started taking my book seriously, before I got lost in details, I had to find a way to think of the job. It was instinctive to want to know what degree of power I had to focus on what scale of surface. The process is worth going through because although we will perform differently from each other, the base complications of writing are the same, only the outcomes differ according to levels of art and work. I'd already figured out that finished writing wouldn't drip from my fingertips; I needed a mindset that would carry me through the job of making it flow as if it had. By the time I'd been through the headfuck of deciding whether it was better to imagine it an easy job and ignore any issues, or a hard job and agonise over everything, I realised I needed one guiding principle to govern my efforts, and it was the karate chop.

The aiming point had to be beyond the target, so that the work of a first book had its pressure load spread over a wider area. I had to not only commit to finishing something but to finishing a full-length novel. Better still, I had to think of the novel as a beginning, it would be a trilogy of novels. It made the first effort an opening gambit. In terms of the effort I needed to expend, it should be everything I had, day after day, month after month, climbing through targets. I didn't know how hard it would be, I couldn't know – and like all of us I went in without guarantees that I wasn't wasting my time. For all I knew I could still be sat at those pages today. It's to say that it took a decisive thought, a commitment to something specific, and it was to punch through the job.

In fixing this idea many subordinate issues were also solved. How strong a voice should the narrator have? It should punch through the page. How strong should his desires be? They should punch through him. The idea gave the job a head of steam. It no longer mattered if the work was going to be an immovable object, I was punching through it or breaking myself in the attempt. As for whether to conceive of the job as hard or easy, it meant I did neither, and looking back that was correct. It didn't need that headfuck, or any headfuck. It just needed doing, and all thoughts were spent towards doing it. I closed my eyes, put my best foot forward and punched through it. For comfort there was the benefit of time, which is the writer's advantage. If we had to do our writing at the speed a book is read we'd be in serious shit. As it is, it stays still while we deal with it, waits its turn, and even four books would wait their turn while you performed your martial ballet. The aiming-point trick filtered throughout the work, even became a guideline for the strength of the prose, and translated into good habits while editing. It made me conscious that nothing could be half done, every sentence had to have its punch. Moreover, the idea led me to build stronger situations into the work, positions strong enough to punch out. That meant increased conflict between characters, which is what novels are all about. Not only did conflicts proliferate, they became tougher all the time, and placed more serious consequences in the balance.

It took a lot of planks. But it worked, I finished the book, sketched its two sequels. And in an example of the microcosmic symmetry I allude to all the time the punch was transmitted to my pages. The novel punched its way into the world and kept travelling on through, beyond the aiming point of simply finishing. So now is when to pick your guiding principle. It doesn't matter if the job is easy or hard, we're going to it either way.

Quickly as you can, snatch this pebble from my hand.

I write one page of masterpiece to ninety-one pages of shit. I try to put the shit in the wastebasket.

Ernest Hemingway

8 CRAP

'The responsibility of awful writing' was Hemingway's twist on his own sentence 'the awful responsibility of writing'. As the man who also said, 'First drafts are shit,' he pointed to a truth that's worth exploring before we write a word: it is that if the key to finishing a book is simply sticking with it, then the main challenge for us is to face writing crap. For days, weeks, months, possibly years.

All I liked after writing the first page of *Vernon God Little* was the voice. It had things to say about everything, I could feel it wanting to say them. But I went on to write three hundred pages that didn't make a book. I wrote them in five weeks, in a fever, without looking back. And at the end I still liked the voice – but it hadn't really said anything. Or rather, it had said plenty but nothing else had really happened. The first page had been prompted by a news clip of an American kid being handled into a police car after a high-school shooting; but after three hundred pages there was no shooting in the book. There was no antagonist, no contagonist. There wasn't really a beginning, a middle or an end. It led to a first sober step, which was to acknowledge that the pages didn't add up to a book. As much as I liked certain parts, it didn't express the feeling I set out with. I had to think of it as a work in progress and learn how to write it. Most of the best writing was already in its mud, the artwork of the book, its spirit – but it was a pile of throbbing organs without a skeleton, the expressions by themselves didn't provoke lasting feelings. They wanted setting in situations that did. I sensed this was making hard work of the job, building organs in a pile on the floor. But I soon found advantages to having done it that way. For one thing I would usually find it hard to move on to page two if I didn't like page one. I bet you could wallpaper the planet with books that never got to page two; and there's a circular trap in there, in that some of the energy you need to forge ahead and keep your page count up is generated by forging ahead and pushing your page count up. Even crap gives a sense of achievement when you get to ten, twenty, fifty pages of it. Paradoxical, then, that when you don't get past page one you lose the spur that would move you on to further pages. After that the thing spirals into a bummer and dies while you check your mail for the forty-third time.

Add to this the burden of suggestion that says writing books is a hell of a job, not one for us but for Thomas Hardy. And it is a big job, but it's not the job we think it is, it can be broken into smaller adventures. It's for this reason that it's worthwhile to build a mound of mud and mine it day by day, write like the wind, use different moods, go off on tangents, unload any shit you can. Ignore spelling, grammar, structure. Then take that pile, with bravery and strength, and read it. Get over the cringing and find a glimmer, see what sentence, idea or theme intrigues or excites. Extract it and put it into a new document, then save the first draft and expand on the glimmer, start the process again. If the job gets boring, loosen up, take a tangent, throw in a new character. In this process of decision upon decision about what does and doesn't please us, the work begins to show itself. We show ourselves. If by the end the majority of words and ideas please us, it's our book and our flesh alone. When gems have grown into paragraphs, paragraphs into pages, look again. Identify the part that works best and lift the rest up to it. This is how it climbs.

I wouldn't have written what I wrote if I'd thought about structure and form at the time, my mind would have been scattered. Now my theory for breaking through is that the job is better split and performed backwards. Don't build a house and furnish it but knock up some furniture on a binge and see what architecture it wants. I could only have written the thing this way, with a first pure stage of flight without thinking. It probably came from a fear that I was writing crap, which I largely was. But if that was the case, it worked. That fear shared a dynamic with the act of fleeing, that of not only running because we're afraid but of being afraid because we run. It's worth aspiring to. Obviously if we're writing about a boy going to the river, we make him go to the river, I don't mean we write without an idea; just that we don't have to set it up and see it work. Better ideas will come later, they attract each other.

I've seen that certain types of personality associate with art. Many incline to perfectionism, which in some arises from natural insecurity. It's to say nothing bad: many great writers are at very least that way, some much more so. It's to say that for the sensitive in this way, writing crap can be too painful to bear. Coupled with any dreaminess about the job or one's abilities, any innocence, it can be too sobering to see passion turn into bilge on paper. But if we get over this hurdle, sparkles can begin to appear. Some personalities inclined to write also have a false psychological gamble riding on the job, which can hold us back. A certain part of us bets that we can write, even banks on it; but it's false, the writing we want probably won't appear in the first draft. The wager has us tingling at the page until awkward first results scare us off, and with seeming good reason, if we're writing crap. It's one of the stranger phenomena that a perfect sentence in the mind can become something else on the page, it diffracts. We come to the task with a sense that strong feelings and ideas should by themselves turn into vigorous writing, but they rarely do when we start out. It could be that they do with practice, but I wouldn't bank on it.

Some others of us write well enough but are persistently unhappy with what we write, which is a lesser problem, as at least the work gets agonisingly polished. Still others become so enchanted with our first words that the page becomes a sacred cow that we can't move forward with or change. The solution to that is a solution to much of art: find a way to not give a shit. Writing is our bitch, it's robust, it's plastic. Against all the monkeys the job can put on our backs stands one truth: it's not a book until it's finished, and finishing it means getting past the monkeys.

If you watch a dieter breaking their diet you'll see that they eat things quickly. They gobble them before they can stop themselves, before the internal arguments, before the shame. Guiltily and fast: that's how to approach a first draft if writing crap would otherwise pain you. A free writer is not something you are but a place you can go. Good writing happens after a climb, draft after draft into clear, thin air where things finally gel. After a fever-ish time, fatigued and adhered to your pages, you cross a kind of sound barrier beyond which everything is exhila-rating. It can take a while, isn't guaranteed, and we often can't stay long – but it's our Shangri-La, and once you're there, you're there. Centuries ago it was a job of literary critics to interpret facets of a work which the writer was unaware of, because when we write this way a state can arise where we flow with perfect lucidity, a state not of thinking but of being; Cicero's *motus animi continuus*. It doesn't happen when we're fretting over a sentence but when we chase an idea without thinking. The *motus* doesn't come often, don't sit waiting for it – but it's out there, a kind of flying, a performance, and one good spell can make a book shout.

As for sitting in front of a page waiting for it to sparkle, we can't, we have to go after it with weapons, and these ideas are them. If we do just sit around, neuroscience promises new creative brain-cycles every ninety min-utes, so that should be as long as we have to wait. But we shouldn't wait. Chasing lucidity can be draining, sleep-less, it can emotionally absent us from the world, make us fastidious, grumpy and paranoid. But the jitters come from overstimulation, from an excitement as genuine as any life-and-death adventure. A spell of that can hook us for ever.

To start the climb: speed. Don't look down. The writers we studied at school had less temptation to stop and correct a typewritten or handwritten page, they had to keep going. Keep a note of your page or word count, watch it grow like an investment. Amp yourself up. When we do things this way a phenomenon comes to bear which justifies our approach beyond getting over the crap factor: *art*. You don't have to be a magical thinker to know that in fiction some of what we write will crystallise for reasons we can't explain. Wait and see how hard it is to write the synopsis of a work after it's finished compared to before it's begun. What's the book about? We should know, we wrote it – yet there's a sense that in its writing it became something else.

A sense that it came into a life of its own.

Man is tormented by no greater anxiety than to find someone quickly to whom he can hand over that great gift of freedom with which the ill-fated creature is born.

Fyodor Dostoevsky

9 FLOCK

I found myself in a taxi with Tobias, a German photographer and broadcaster. We had decided to go to a cemetery on the dusty outskirts of Monterrey, northern Mexico, a sprawling desert city under snowless alps, lately a reluctant cog in Mexico's gang wars. Tobias turned up with a grin, a bucket of chemicals, a historical camera like a wooden nesting box with a hood, and a toy gun.

'We have nine minutes and thirty-one seconds to get there,' he tells the taxi driver. Apparently that's when the sun will sink behind the Sierras, he arrived a day early and worked it out. He stares at the driver till he accepts it's no joke 'because Germans don't joke'. The gist of the day is that, years before, Tobias had a notion to photograph and interview writers in cemeteries. For the sake of art, for the sake of reflection. He felt it would frame them in an unusually meaningful space. The idea was that authors would choose a cemetery significant to them, and so we corresponded for three years, across various continents, hunting a time and a graveyard to meet at. I didn't have a particular place in mind, I was spoilt for choice.

Across those years Tobias photographed Margaret Atwood, Jonathan Franzen, Annie Proulx – who brilliantly chose dinosaur fossils in a cave for her portrait – and dozens of others, travelling as far afield as New Zealand and Iceland. Some writers posed by family gravestones, others paid homage to the monuments of the great, some refused to even enter a cemetery when the day came.

Tobias wasn't sponsored for this. There was no book contract, no gallery waiting back home. He lugged his old camera and bucket around for love and art, a man possessed. It's just Tobias: never touches alcohol but admits to half a kilo of chocolate a day. You have to like him.

We kept track of each other until a shoot with Dean Koontz took Tobias to California, just a border away from Mexico. By the time he went, the years had seen the toll from Mexico's violence reach fifty thousand souls. Suddenly there was a bigger reason to stand in a cemetery than any personal loss of mine. So I dressed in black, he grabbed his bucket of salts, and we went to the hub of a death toll.

We have four minutes and six seconds to get there.

The driver races through tattered neighbourhoods as Tobias chats. 'Anyway,' he ventures, 'here can't be as dangerous as Ciudad Juárez?' At the time Ciudad Juárez has the highest murder rate in the world. The driver considers it for a moment before tilting his hand from side to side: 'Yes and no.' When Tobias first asked me what he should bring to Monterrey apart from his bucket and camera, I said a gun. It was a joke, for fuck's sake. Germans do joke, after all, because he brought this plastic toy that I was meant to pose with, in a town with probably more machine guns than Afghanistan. An assailant could have died laughing. We stash the toy.

Our destination finally looms ahead, just in time for the last rays of sun. Tobias shoots me against the mountains on old Polaroid plates, stripping the negatives off to soak in his bucket of salts. He says this large-format film was discontinued years ago, he scoured Berlin for all the old stock he could find, every last pack. But what stands out from our sweltering date among headstones and crypts is that we eventually came upon a freshly dug grave. Its tenant hadn't arrived, it was an open hole.

Tobias's face lit up. 'Why don't you get in?'

'Because it's not my hole.' I looked into the pit.

'Are you afraid?'

A strange moment. I mean, the hole wasn't dangerous or sinister in itself, it belonged to nobody yet, and I could have climbed back out after the picture. It even had a ledge halfway down, for someone to climb in and out. And yet.

In a hot breeze we looked down into the hole, someone's last resting place, and maybe lived the moment, had the thoughts and feelings we were there to have. Was the occupant even dead yet? Were graves dug pre-emptively? And anyway, weren't we standing with a ticket in the same lottery as anyone?

'Fuck it,' picking up a rock from the diggings I went down onto the ledge and stood there as if interrupted in the process of burying myself.

It's a whimsical way into the point of this chapter, which is that *like attracts like*. The observation is that birds of a feather flock together on many levels, possibly on all levels, and that it's pertinent to writing and to being a writer: our work carries our feather and calls its own flock to it. Once we bear this dynamic in mind we can also apply it to our characters' worlds. It's as if people and their experiences leave traces, spread tendrils of code that probably account for our sense of Kismet and luck. We transmit attractants and repellents that influence the world of our daily operations unbeknownst to us. It's not magic, we know that our chemistry and psychology are coded. But there's more to it. Our interest as writers is in what brings counterparts together, aside from their shared interest in something, or their mutual goal. On one level we're simply talking about the focus effect: like the day you buy a Maserati and suddenly start seeing them everywhere. That effect is a damned useful tool in art and writing, one you can sit back and count on. From the moment we make a decision about a theme or story, it focuses a lens that throws relevant material to mind until we end up inhabiting a world where many things pertain to or are repelled from our story. Dialogue overheard on the street, characters walking with their troubles and foibles, settings, moods and anecdotes all start to feed the world of our idea in some way. We only have to make the decision for the effect to begin. A book with an ironic narrator brings ironies to our attention, a book on madness pitches madness if not makes us mad. If we already have a start on paper, all the better, if we're just winging notes for a future idea, great; but even if we don't, things will parade through a prism of our current ideas, once we admit them. Which effect I figure also accounts for how fucked-up people can get over their deeply held beliefs, whatever they might be; they filter and pull vindications from the scenes around like filings to a magnet, until their conclusions are obvious to them. So then it's true that we become what we focus on. We inhabit our focus and it shapes us.

There's also a mysterious part to this observation, one I find self-evident, though of course it will appear so now because I'm focusing on it (just to give the damn sentence more chain than it can swim with): it is that once an idea gains focus, not only do our observations grow relevant to it but outside agents of it are also drawn to us. And the deeper into the idea we get, the more they come along. Fred and Rosemary West won't have come together by ticking the serial-killer box on a dating form, but after being attracted to each other's codes and precursors, invisible strands of instinct. As if in our opening a window in some direction, other receptors sense it and reach inside. Our choice of story, however spontaneous it might seem, probably flows from an existing instinctive relationship with its theme, expressed as a like or an interest, whether we know and admit it or not. The impact on our childhood of seeing a grandfather's death might have led to a certain curiosity in the direction of death, which led us to cast a certain hue over the theme – and once our decision is made to write it, that hue grows material in the world around us as the idea grows its flesh.

That 'following wind' effect may or may not attend all decisions in life, but many say it does: Christians say it does when the motives are godly, entrepreneurs say it does if you kick ass, pessimists say it does blow more shit your way. But when you're in the business of gathering pictures and flavours from life to build other worlds with in writing, the following wind is a real effect. Make the decision and watch an idea begin to furnish itself, awake and asleep. For the same reason, a book you don't actively work on today is still being written in the background, no time is lost.

As for birds of a feather flocking together, the way we end up meeting counterparts can be uncanny. Look around. At the extreme, for example, while it's shocking when someone gets beaten by a partner in a relationship, there are plenty of innocent people being beaten in successive relationships, again and again, often by partners just as surprised to be doing the beating. Something else is at work in our connections. Certain flowers are open to certain bees and they know each other without thinking. If you're histrionic, if you're paranoid, if you're dependent you will probably inhabit a world at least partly peopled by counterparts. People with demons seem to live in worlds of others with demons, or their opposite counterparts, which can sometimes mean bigger demons still; and when you write, those feathered friends will also code your writing because no matter what you consciously build into a work it will have an aura. You can then find that others who live with, or understand, or are interested by or drawn to that shadow will especially warm to it. If you're published, your agents, publishers, some of your fans will know the taste of your shadow, it will ping to them as surely as a beacon to a ship. And there can come a time when you look around and find yourself surrounded. In writing out your *duende* you've called another multitude to you.

Maybe then the real writing begins.

Bear this effect in mind both inside a narrative and in life, in the connections you make. If you're a maniac you will find maniacs, and not just by projection. It's particularly relevant to published writers because of the way books find their way to readers. A good rejection letter will tell you that your submission might be a fine book, but that for an agent to run with it they must feel an exciting personal connection, which in your case is lacking; and they're not kidding. No matter its subject, form or style, your book will have an aura, so that in seeking a strong connection with someone else it must on some level draw out your like.

It's a useful idea in itself, a phenomenon that can feed compelling attractions and symbioses between characters in the writing. Imagine the coded dialogue between maniac counterparts on a first date, or between a couple conditioned by different fears. She asks for a table away from the pond – she survived a near-drowning as a child; he hunches protectively over his food – he was raised with bullies in an orphanage.

Tuning our receivers to the subtle threads that condition and connect us is a cool way to the heart of what makes a story real, threads that live in the oblique and unspoken, that roam the gap between what's done and meant. It makes for smarter writing than simply throwing a character who loves blondes into a room with a blonde. With oblique dialogue and action we can infer why the judge secretly loves his chauffeur, why the mother wants her son's best friend, why the abuser needs the same kind of victim. Sure, it's psychology – but we don't have to understand or explain it, we just have to write how it looks to us.

Tobias invoked a playful following wind after coaxing me at toy-gunpoint into an open grave. When I returned from Monterrey I was offered a chance to write something with a supernatural twist. I buried myself in it, filled it with Kismet and death, and delivered it to the publisher on the day that I attended the opening of Tobias's cemetery exhibition. A coffee-table book was published and launched at the Museum for Sepulchral Culture, an impressive German venue dedicated to funeral paraphernalia and death.

I arrived to find Tobias looking dapper, busy with last-minute details. The museum is a spectacular space on a cliff overlooking the home town of the brothers Grimm. A few hundred people turned up to the show and Tobias was acclaimed there amidst the coffins, urns and headstones. Over a glass of wine we mingled afterwards with some of the guests. One smart gentleman approached me, and after a while told me that he was an undertaker. Apparently undertakers visit museums of death in their free time. I had to smile.

'You know, Pierre,' he mused, 'when I was young all I wanted to be was a clown. Instead I ended up being a funeral director.' He chuckled and sipped his wine: 'Now I know they're the same job.'

The night began to sparkle with irony and coincidence, a gentle following wind. After some drinks I accompanied Tobias to an Italian restaurant for the show's post-mortem.

A couple of guests from the audience tagged along, one of them a college professor. I caught Tobias smiling as we ambled down the road, also shaking his head at the night. If I found the Kismet teasing after only having my picture taken in a grave, Tobias must have been drowning in it. I broached this question of decisions and their following wind as the doctor and his partner drew alongside.

'I have to leave Germany,' said Tobias. 'After three years on this project I'm now only known as "the cemetery guy". Next month I'm moving to South America. I found a place with cocoa trees in the garden. I can't even pick up the phone any more, it's just "cemetery guy, cemetery guy, cemetery guy".'

'Don't even talk to me about answering the phone,' sighed the doctor. 'I have to use my middle name. I get the same thing over and over.'

Tobias and I looked at him.

'My surname is Frankenstein.'

I hate to advocate drugs, alcohol, violence, or insanity to anyone, but they've always worked for me.

Hunter S. Thompson

10 DRUGS

All things that become familiar go through progressive seasons. We can look back on the season of their discovery and marvel at how different the thing was – a new neighbourhood, a friend, a job, a hobby, a love – then its paradigms shifted and spun till we were tattered by it. Some of this lies in our simply growing familiar, trading dynamic quality for static; but within that I feel there are seasons.

Looking back over my experience with drugs I see that their effects went through a series of seasons. Like Alice in Wonderland, through little doors and never back again. Every one was a world of its own, and for the first time I take stock of what each produced creatively, if anything. For instance, the creative output from my first ever joint was saying 'yeah' a lot. In fact 'yeah' pretty much covered the first few joints. That first world was one of inward focus, monitoring effects and comparing them to so-called reality. By about the fifth joint I was in a car sharing the experience with good friends. We didn't come to feel we were Jesus, but we got close to being his wingmen. Like divers hauling mysteries back from the deep, we wrote the things we said onto cigarette packets in order to laugh later at how bent they sounded.

Except they weren't from the deep. We were talking shit. It just felt like the deep. Still, it was a new world – and who doesn't love a new world?

The next season, a year or so down the track, was one of ritual delusion. Of staking all your heart on the first hit, going to any lengths to secure it, waking strangers for it in the night; then realising it wasn't such a big a deal. But still saying 'yeah' and 'wow' and playing at having achieved your essential state, while anxiously calculating the next hit. This was the season when the drug world became an establishment, of rituals, of enabling language and lore, of hierarchies of users according to consumption and panache. Our spliff-rolling styles were established and a mentality entrenched which disdained sobriety, and hence reality. But in hindsight the experience of the day's first hit during that season was, after a minute, one of disappointment that it was over. There was no output at all that season – but there was good talk of it.

Following this something must have clicked, because the focus shifted from sitting around waiting for the drug to fly us away. Now we went out and used it as a licence to adventure. Abandoned amusement parks, racing our cars, living night as day and day as night. We still said 'yeah', but less now. We just watched things, watched ourselves do them. We communicated more with our eyes. The physical output was still zero but we were living big, and that meant we were taking on fuel, testing ourselves, calibrating for a big life. We couldn't have done it on milkshakes.

By the next season, fledged by that activity, we added new drugs. We no longer sought shit to make doing nothing seem amazing; now we wanted shit to make us amazing doing something. *Speed.* And so we sped through the season. We were still on a road to nowhere, but faster now, which brought its own sense of purposeful travel. There was still almost zero creative output of any note, but it no longer felt that way. There would be one thing – a painting, a design, a plan, or just some random contact – that we used as a banker. And we banked on it, without being so stupid as to actually try to do it. Apart from that we were an ants' nest of projects in development, with people we knew we couldn't trust and would never see again. Our currency was bullshit.

The next season was precarious because we got involved with women. Drugs, to the heights we had been used to them, now had to shrink into the spaces between girls. It wasn't that the women were so much against drugs, it was that they disdained us when we were bent, probably feeling excluded from the pack. Disdain wasn't good feedback for us, so time was split between women and 'business'. Business meant getting bent with the pack and feeling like the ants' nest again. That's what mansion-dwellers do, the world over. It's impossible to approach something with the right vigour when it leads to a smaller place than you already inhabit. If it also comes with a risk, plain forget it. By this time, drugs-wise, we were old hands at dosages and effects, which is a large habitat that doesn't automatically suggest trading for a job stacking shelves. Shit needs to be automatic in youth, we're not going to play chess over everything.

The next season brought a chill breeze. The first of the pack was dead. A lack of chess. The remainder of us split up to try our bullshit on the wider world. We were in different countries facing different realities flowing from adulthood. I couldn't identify the breeze at the time, but looking back I see that it came from an opening door. Reality's door, whatever the fuck it was apart from hateful. The only thing that could buffer the chill was more drugs. But they felt lonelier. They were a movie compared to the theatre of earlier seasons. A toke here, a line there. Drink, smoke, ha, ha, ha. And this was the dangerous season. Because the more the door opened, the more drugs it took to warm up. And the more lonely drugs you took, the wider the door opened. You come to realise that you are the only physical creative output of years.

Then you get sucked through the door.

After a solid kicking, then a break, the next season was a tentative return to the tiny exhilarations of beer. Shaving, being polite, and gentle beer. A reorientation. Wearing pressed clothes. Creative output actually rose. It rose like never before but it was timid and conservative. It was a dance with current standards, nothing new. This brought its own chill, which gathered into a gale.

That conservatism and conformity led to the frustration of a dog. So the next season was a lusty pillage of the first season's ethos. There had been something in its innocence, curiosity and gall that was essential, something that had been lost and overlaid with sensible ideas of the kind governments propose as guidelines. A joint relit a spark, stronger drink, other things, if they happened by. I recovered my balls. And now the wind had real strength, I angled my sails into it. Now ideas were treated as a job. I recorded them and they fell into a longer work until the work was its own drug and it was impossible to get bent on anything else.

It was a weaning, but all the seasons before had predicted its taste.

This chapter fits here because if you're going to use drugs, do it to write that first story. Drugs work for the art but not so much the craft. Any job of writing obviously relies on coffee, tobacco and at least one bender a week to blow any nesting conservatism away. But some can also benefit from drugs. If you don't already take them don't start taking them for writing, there are too many seasons to go through. But if you take them, this is how they can work. Again, I write as though we're all maniacs, it's not true, there are completely ascetic writers. But we all seem to binge on something, if only moderation. As for you and this piece, I have to presume that you have an inner maniac. Your maniac is now useful, contrary to current guidelines. The maniac and the drugs can be useful – used at the right moment.

To look at drug use and other opting-out mechanisms such as psychological disorders we need to touch on the ideas said to underlie them, and the school of thought currently in charge – one we're strangely fond of, making it exceptionalist by our own endorsement – is the one broadly saying that behind most compulsion, neurosis, drug reliance and unhappiness is a deep-rooted sense that we're no good. If we're errant it's because we somehow think we're no good. If we're meek it's because we feel we're no good. If we're arrogant we're compensating for being no good. If we're fat we're buffering ourselves from being no good. If we're too skinny we're trying to lose whatever makes us no good. If we drink we're trying to forget we're no good. Overachiever: no good. Underachiever: no good. Indifferent achiever: no good.

The argument quickly vanishes up the arsehole of philosophy because we have to define what good is, and, more pertinently, ask if anyone at all is realistically able, or should even be inclined to be that way, whatever it is. But the no-good theory just has a ring to it. As a culture we love and use it, and if it wasn't true at the outset we've sure made it so by now. Face it: we're just no damn good.

If we take this as true, any practical use of the idea needs us to define how it affects us; and I think its effects lie in issues of vulnerability and power. Which – here's the thing – it seems to share with the act of writing. I stop short of linking insecurity with writing, but I'm inclined to. Writing a book not only gives power, the power to define worlds, people, and change them at a stroke, but in battling our vulnerabilities to seize, wield and withstand that power we must also redraw ourselves. The pen is also a pantograph. In the necessity of setting boundaries for characters, in having to scour our consciences for outcomes, we're forced to think and feel at once on a broad scale. Some will say that being a police officer, a government minister, a teacher imposes the same effects, but it doesn't; those jobs thoughtfully speculate on human outcomes but their power is limited by strict procedure, precisely to shut out the gambles and whims that infect our writing. They may impact other lives, but only we get naked and design a world from scratch.

So if we buy into the school of no good maybe writing is an emancipation from some kind of powerlessness, if only the powerlessness of all creatures. Perhaps it's a new upbringing. Maybe it's proof to ourselves and the world that we're OK, if not good. Or it could be an empty cry in the dark. Only one thing seems clear: if you have shadows they will send their demons when you start to write seriously. If they think you're shit, they'll come to prove it. If you set out to write from feelings you'll especially disturb them and they may try to kill you. If you play it safe and write commercially they will merely try to stop you from finishing – if social networking and lifestyle don't beat them to it.

However our experience is, the demons that come are by many definitions our only challenge in life. Scaring them into view is to our advantage, though it can be unpleasant; stuck in an arena together we can befriend or slay them. And there are few arenas as well furnished for inner combat as writing, where you invent your own weapons and outcomes. If with the faintest tremble you suspect I've identified you here, then this book is dedicated to you. If you read this with bemusement, on the other hand, then the rest of us dedicate our works to you because this is what some of us are like.

If at some point in life we have opted out and held ourselves back, or if our opting out has been solely or also through drugs, it puts us in an outside place, and outside places are the playgrounds of all art. We can use that. Drugs therefore qualify. The side effects of disorder and drugs, such as distrust and even paranoia, can suddenly also be useful. Distrust is a great writer's tool, whether it comes from personal philosophy or sensitivity to bullshit, it makes us dissect situations for ourselves, lets us see the unspoken transactions and implications of the everyday, all of which makes for lifelike writing. It even works when we're wrong: because the details still carry the scent of real shadows. And the world is more shadow than light, there's more power among neurotics than among reasonable people. It's easier in the world for North Korea to happen than Sweden, and in some meas- ure our writing will reflect that state of affairs, even if our work becomes Sweden by the end.

We're writing for people like us – that is, ourselves.

To drugs and their practical application to writing, we should start by throwing out all populist hysteria. No one who sucks prescribed Ritalin, Elavil or Prozac can throw a stone at weed and ecstasy. No one who gets knee-walking at Christmas parties can finger cocaine and speed as the root of any evil. We should accept that we've always been an intoxicated culture. The wheel of fortune spins from time to time onto new prohibitions but the fact that they come and go, unlike murder, makes them temporal ideas. Less than a century ago we could buy heroin and cocaine in department stores. You could buy them and more in over-the-counter preparations at the chemist, many aimed at children. We fought two world wars on them. And times haven't changed: since the med- ical-health complex discovered that GDP rises with every doctor's visit there isn't a panacea held back from con- sumer markets. While aghast at the thought of 'drugs', my mother lost weight on prescribed speed and handled difficult days with Valium. My father, a straight man, was fed amphetamines every day by the government to help him pilot heavy bombers. Of course, the missing word in all this is 'recreational', they will say the drugs were tools, not licensed to be run amok with on the streets. But neither is writing recreation. In our job we can now say: they are tools, not for running amok with either, except on a page. So fuck off.

Writing is heavy bombing.

MUSIC

Starting with the heaviest drug, the jury is out on whether listening to music while writing is a good idea. I love music and used to listen to it while writing, but in the end I made a sad discovery: I was susceptible enough that it became a soundtrack to what I wrote, which made the work seem better than it was. My feelings were being stirred by the soundtrack more than the words, and I attributed some of the feeling to them. I had to decide to write in silence. It works, and the music of sentences and passages is clearer. Be especially careful when writing under pressure: angst promotes music for inspiration, then you find yourself in the cold light of day reading crap that only looked good along with music. Having said this, music during a first draft can work, before the arrangement of words matters too much. Also a first draft and final polish can use speed music, in the same way a tank commander uses heavy metal.

SEX

A question that runs straight to classical thought. The idea is that sexual and creative energies are one and the same, so if we spend them on sex it leaves less for creative action. It's an old idea that's still at least suspected. It might be true, it's another one we like, we imagine the bristling energies spent in orgasm being a power that we could spend in other ways, as if it's just damming there waiting to paint or fuck. The mechanics of hunger and satisfaction probably make it true by themselves in the sense that we're less ruthless when sated. Writing is also the work of a clam, building nacre around some irritant. So to some extent we have to preserve the irritant. It could be best to write conflict before sex, when the future is tangy, and write resolutions and reflections in the salty calm aftermath.

ALCOHOL

Between us and our livers. If you can drink and write at the same time, go ahead and 'write drunk, edit sober'. I can't. Not because I write incoherently, although I also can drunk – but because a drink strangely distracts me from the page. For me the key to using high times is to wing notes from them – on napkins, cigarette papers – and bring them to work later. It becomes a custom and occasionally yields gold in images and ideas. Other times what you've scribbled brings back the memory, but the buzz you were trying to capture has faded, too nuanced to survive. Whether you do or don't drink and write – try it and compare – the real boon of alcohol is in the hangover.

Next day after the pastries, the coffee, any spinning, when life returns and the day opens onto a sunlit plain, we can write like the people we won't be for many years. Wisdom, altruism and microsensitivity can blow through a hangover. Our work will have sections that need those qualities, and we should plan to visit them then. Write violence and conflict before a drink – resolve them from the bosom of a hangover.

CAFFEINE

We want to be perky for the job. Caffeine is the legal way, plus cheaper and tastier than Benzedrine. Just beware of burnout. Tea or coffee can get you started but I promise once the job's engine is running you will have more than enough stimulus to carry on. You'll twitch just as much on internal power, a few chapters into a book you might find that sleep is being destroyed by the writing alone. Management is key. Again, cut loose for the first draft and final push, throttle back in between.

CANNABIS

Weed is a writerly drug. Not rollercoaster but chill-out strength. It is the drug of choice for staring at a blank page and watching stories grow in tangents. Just the tip of a joint will ripple thoughts, paddle the mind out behind breaking concerns to where things play. Not every part of the job can use it, it's for first drafts and snags needing unexpected thinking. Once the piece has life the effects can mess up critical thought, so there's a time to dream and a time to be fastidious. You'll gather that a first draft can be launched with all guns blazing; but a natural effect of its coming to life is amping you beyond comfortable stimulation. If you ever suffered the horrors of a drug, such as anxiety or runaway thoughts, they will be the first sign. You know you're onto something when you're electric without external props. I'm convinced it's the reason artists go mad.

I recommend hash over grass, it's mellower and pays respect to Baudelaire.

COCAINE AND SPEED

The same goes for these times ten in terms of ampage. I'd also be wary of setting up a reward system with coke that gets us hooked in order to write. If we wrote well on it at first, it could keep us in fear of never doing it again without the drug. Then the solution could only be more. If you go for it I'd say try to finesse it into a perfect routine: open the page at the same time every day, lay out the lines, and write to a specific target every time. Maybe keep it brief, train yourself to go crazy at that time, then retire after as little as half an hour and no more than three hours, which seems to be the average maximum among a host of big writers. Substitute espressos in leaner times. As for street speed, we want to be alert without grinding our teeth. I would find it too coarse, too distracting for what we're trying to do. Likewise, amphetamines can surge and fall, which leaves you waiting for the downer, although they were the drug of choice for plenty of writers back in the day. Those writers probably avoided the downer by taking more.

ECSTASY

I'm inspired to think this might be a playwright's drug. Shifts in affect between characters, alternating warm and stark dialogue, poignant spaces all come to mind with MDMA and its family. As a feel-good drug it probably joins music in posing the danger that amazing feelings get attributed to the writing. Still, nothing some rainy daylight won't cure. If you can stay still and put your romance on the page, write a play.

OPIUM

If you take it in the vein you're either going to write a labyrinthine saga or nothing at all. There's a test for it: where you place a hundred thousand words in a book, and what those words are, opens a spectrum from the worst book ever written to the best as yet unwritten. The words can assemble around any story you're trying to tell, and the odds of any other work ever being the same are beyond the number of atoms in the universe to calculate. The question is: what will you write? If you can answer this on smack, you're good to go. Chasing the dragon or making a joint of it could be more lyrical. In quantity this will be a drug for the first draft, or else a long book about your carpet. Otherwise make notes for after rehab.

HALLUCINOGENS

Not even for a first draft. Tripping expands the writer, not the writing. So probably best to get this out of the way before sitting down to work. On its trailing edge a trip might shimmer like a hangover and be useful as it dies, but it's experimental territory. The leading edge is too fast, and the peak will shake itself free from any purposeful work. Make notes, by all means, whenever the walls are still.

FATIGUE

If we're in the business of other worlds, it's best to go there with faculties intact. The most useful intoxicants for writing are already in the brain. Fatigue is a sweet distancing device that also lures out strong feelings – I don't mean tiredness, an earlier state we have to pass through, but the proper shiny-eyedness at the back of it. As readers we talk of losing ourselves in a book, and books more than many things give out what you put in, not just in craft but in energy. Lose yourself in writing and we'll lose ourselves in reading it. Midnight oil. Nothing beats it for charging the glow of a work. Foster it in bursts, the earlier the better, after a big day, a chain of defeats and triumphs, any emotional vortex that can punch you to the page with nothing to lose. Sit festering overnight and through a day, the work speaks differently then, it looks different and we do different things to it. Nerves and censors are shut down. It's an adhesion, a spinning of mental tyres till they burn and melt to the page. We're authorised to test ourselves, rough yourself up. Gather the comforts and triggers, the old clothes, coffee, chocolate and resolve.

And change your luck with them.

ROUTINE

The most common drug among writers, an outcome of the job itself. Most find their way towards training the muse to visit at certain times. Some do it as a matter of discipline, because they find the work uncomfortable and onerous, and others to control their output. But a majority find a rhythm and cast it in stone, sometimes down to the minute of every day. I met an author with kids at home, a noisier life than mine, and she said the only way her writing got done was by going to it before she thought of anything else. Before breakfast, before dressing, before speaking. It seems many writers get it out of the way early, to a target of time or words, and some swear the muse visits at those times. When their target is met, the same writers use discipline to get up from the job, leaving them keen with anticipation for the rest of the day.

In the end the only real drug is our work. Whatever our daily habits, however uncomfortable we find the job, whatever tricks we have to play on ourselves to return, whatever other madness we deal with – we foster an addiction to our pages.

Closing this I can already hear the next-of-kin reacting, those who lost a loved one to drugs. This writing pays no disrespect, it's a factual reflection for people who assess their own risks and run their own lives. Having called the written word the last free space for discourse, having told everyone to kill their censors, I can't now write half a book owing to the sensitivities of the times. Many people try to write, but this is for people who wonder if they're writers. I still wonder. In short, writing attracts certain people and some will do drugs. This part was for them. Consistent with our time and place, social proof is currently everything in writing. It means you're a piss-tank until you write your masterpiece, then you're an eccentric.

Either way, you're in good company: Proust worked on opium powder and sedatives, Graham Greene on amphetamines, Balzac on four dozen coffees a day, W. H. Auden on amphetamines and sedatives, Sartre on ten times the adult dose of amphetamines, plus alcohol, barbiturates and two packs of cigarettes. A swathe of writers worked only in bed, and Schiller couldn't write without rotting apples nearby.

Which is to say: there's space enough for us in there.

PART TWO
GOING EQUIPPED

What matters is that my novel should cover everything.

If it does not work I will hang myself.

Fyodor Dostoevsky

11 CHARACTERS

I hung out with older people when I was young. They had more 'raisins in their oatmeal', to use one of their own sayings for a well-furnished mind. They also seemed to die less than contemporary friends. There was safety in them, and nourishment, between bouts of reckless times.

One crew was a bullfight pack. Certain regional neighbours in Spain had bailed out of the USA to chase a Hemingwayesque dream of cowhide, cigar smoke and sweat, with all the metaphysics it implied, of honour and culture and *duende*. Like a daisy-chain through Granada, Malaga, Ronda and down the coast, the aficionados became my friends, although I was less into cowhide. They were arts people, free-thinking, curious, often dramatic and always fun. David, a Czech-American from California, had run away at seventeen to become a bullfighter in Mexico. Now in his forties he was one of the younger aficionados in the gang, and still looked and moved like a bullfighter. He came with the most striking Iberian figure of a wife, also imported from California to show the Iberians what Goya had missed. She was someone behind whose ear a rose should have grown naturally. When she once attracted flirting from an Italian film crew, David was so incensed that he disowned all Italians for life. I stumbled on that little thread after hearing him call Michelangelo a glorified illustrator and Frank Sinatra a fat Italian criminal.

His wife Sara was a fine artist, and he had also ended up painting rather than fighting bulls, in the days of the matadors Ordóñez and El Cordobés. But like the folks mystically drawn to Devils Tower mountain in *Close Encounters of the Third Kind*, the bullfight was just an icon for a deeper pull, to all things Iberian, to a post-Franco Andalusia where hearts, families and towns remained split and at war. It was a second wave inspired by those who wrote back from the civil war, and where that wave touched the southern coast it alloyed with expats inspired by Michener's *The Drifters*, a tale that made you want to sit in empty rooms smoking hash in the days before mass tourism fucked the coast, back when not wearing a tie on a weekday made you a bum.

I suppose I was kind of a third wave, too young to have been inspired by those histories, but inspired by who was inspired by them. In the same way that by the age of twelve I had felt the Second World War as a memory of my own via my parents' stories, this period was also a wormhole into Franco's Spain. I absorbed it by osmosis from those who absorbed it from those who were there. In that way, without knowing it, I was furnishing myself not only with a knowledge of history but its feeling and taste and smell.

The only way to live beyond our time.

Down the coast near the remains of Michener's Torre-molinos lived a sixtysomething blonde heiress who chain-smoked and trembled and fell in desperate love like a child with a succession of banderilleros and picadors, maybe the odd matador too. Every time I saw her she would clutch my arm, push beer-bottle glasses in my face and quiver through her latest heartbreak.

'He hasn't called! Should I call him? He hinted that he would call, but was it just a ploy to get me to call him? Would it make me look too needy? Oh my God, oh Christ, oh shit, if only the bastard would call! Why doesn't he call? You'd call me, wouldn't you? Christ, maybe I'll just call him.'

This for a pink-suited man she had handed a card to over the ringside barrier at a bullfight. Her house had a pulse timed to her attendance at *corridas*, and seemed to pound with drama after every one.

There was another small inscrutable British lady, like a Russian doll in a headscarf. She wore massive sunglasses day and night, and lorded it over my humble gang of aficionados, not only because she had been there first, even before Michener, but because she had actually had a glossy, authoritative book published in the sixties about a great matador. She held court in cafés and restaurants, icily aloof and monosyllabic until she was drunk, after which she was a cuddly waif. I gave her a lift to her house one night and she stumbled in to get me a copy of her book. Someone else in the car warned me not to take it, as the thing had been out of print for ages and she had already squandered all her own copies on new friends.

Everyone down this coast was some kind of escapist. All seemed to be running from something, maybe just from themselves.

It suited me. I was a runner with the best of them.

I was already familiar with the bullfight, having grown up near the world's largest bullring. But in Spain I attended a *corrida* with the aficionados and absorbed new explanations and reflections on the theatre of death. From the women I learned its links to Mithraism, its ancient moorings to the symbolism of man versus woman, the man being the bull; from the men I heard the mechanics of unfair advantage, the laws and protocols that exhausted, irritated and crippled the bull in readiness for its end. I learned that by Spanish law a fighting bull was forbidden from seeing a standing human for five years until its fateful encounter in the ring. I learned that until recently many more horses than bulls died in the ring, gored without armour. I learned that the matador had to make his kill within a certain number of minutes, as that was the time it took for a bull to learn that the cape was a decoy; and I watched a matador walk with his dying beast, hugging its useless neck and crying like a child.

It was hard shit. Those people lived the *corrida* as it must've been lived a century ago, revelling in both creatures' courage, artistry and pomp, in our raw humanity naked and stinking around predictable if not certain death.

Because humanity has never been innocent.

Something to note if you're a people watcher: the most revealing insights are on the fringes, not at the core. A zealot leader might be a study in zeal, but a broader spectrum of colours will flash from his followers. If we were writing about bullfights it might occur to us to make a bullfighter the protagonist; but these characters would suit us better, the bullfighter is simpler than the effect he has.

Another friend of the aficionados was Richard, an Oklahoma Christian so reborn and fundamental that he didn't go to church, 'Because there are no Christians there.' I first heard of him through an anecdote where he sat across a table getting pious and prickly with David over religion; and at the height of Richard's tirade, eyes ablaze, brows aloft, one of David's teeth popped out into his hand. Such was the power of Richard's God.

Richard had abandoned a lifelong career as a rocket scientist, plus a wife, a grown child and an affluent future, after hearing God's objective voice. It commanded him to Spain to be a poor neighbour in an apartment where he translated his own scriptures, adopted body odour and grew faithful. I knew him as an affable, lilting presence with the eyebrows of Isaiah. When you opened your door to his knock he would cock sideways at the waist, wave jazz-hands and sing 'Hola!' as if you might not want to see him. He came to share loneliness, drink Coke and talk about something or nothing. We once walked through the lounge of a café where a television caught our eye. It played the live countdown to a Space Shuttle mission. Richard had worked on the Space Shuttle programme before hearing God, and I thought it rare luck to stand with him and watch his former project come to life. Even he paused stock-still as the rockets spewed light. But this was the ill-fated *Challenger* mission. We watched it climb away and explode.

'I thought that would happen,' sighed Richard.

As poor as he was, Richard spent some of his purse commissioning David to paint a sensational religious triptych, which he did with great seriousness in oils on three boards. The work would be exhibited down the coast, which meant an aficionado road trip where we hung out on sofas like teens, unfurled our quirks and had our arms gripped over the latest lost love. Between laughter, as is the human way, we all took time to corner one another alone and discuss in low voices the others' spiralling foibles.

Richard even sat through a *corrida* with everyone one Corpus Christi holiday. I don't think he was a fan but he found a chink in his hierarchy of principles to put the road trip and his friends' passions first. So in a shaded seat under the president's box, to the clash of a brass band, there sat this rocket scientist who believed dinosaur bones had been planted to discredit the Bible. He allowed me to talk to him about the dinosaur bones. I heard him admit that he had abandoned critical thought as a matter of belief. Intelligence was fine only as long as it remained an instrument of purpose, which was unquestioning faith. He believed the literal word of the scriptures, which meant that when the day came for the faithful to be raised up to Heaven, they would physically float up off the ground. Over a coffee, from a shower, through oily wads of cemetery earth and from the queue at Madame Tussauds, they would just hover up and keep going.

Our building had a lift. I used to like riding it up with Richard. As we felt it lift off I would gaze at him meaningfully – what if it just kept going? – and he would laugh. As it happened, supporting my theory that what you sip follows in pints, he believed that the world would end in the last August that I knew him. He disposed of his home and possessions for the price of three months' living, paid his few debts. But come September the evil world was still there. He was properly poor and we rode the lift a last time, exchanging glances. He still smiled. That was Richard, still glowing on his path. He had to return to his state to survive. I heard it was a room above someone's garage in the ninth-largest town in Oklahoma.

All these characters gathered for their reasons around the bullfight. Whether they live or not and how much bigger they might be in real life, this is the cast they were on the stage of those days. That's how we can think of our characters: they may come from this and go to that, but they're a cast between the first and last pages of a story, in orbit around each other, exerting their push and pull for as long as they stay. The people above were compelling characters, but they needn't have been for the purposes of writing. Stop and take note of your feelings after reading their sketches: although it's interesting that the rocket scientist thinks dinosaur bones are a conspiracy, that didn't matter here. See if what touched you more wasn't jazz-hands at the door, and riding the lift. Those glimmers are of the man, not his context. Likewise, although it's kinky for the heiress to chase bullfighters, it doesn't matter – what gets us is that she still falls stupidly in love.

Eccentricities make characters.

None of the eccentricities above had to do with the bullfight, or Spain, or those years. Those characters could have been co-workers in a tin mine, they would have behaved the same way on social media. Once you attach a revealing trait to a character in writing, the character begins to live for himself. And once you have a couple of characters, their whims go to work on each other. Add significant quirks sparingly when you set out, then sit back and imagine the characters in different situations. This is how they grow. How would they behave in church, under arrest, in a fight? As they grow you find that they can't be made to do everything you want any more, some things are no longer in their nature; just as in life, the maid won't do the windows. At that point, pile obstacles before her (hire her enemy to do the windows).

The character with the stiffest obstacles in my story must have been Richard. I never saw him again. I later heard that he died back there, above the garage in the ninth-largest town in Oklahoma. I hope his body smashed a hole through the roof on its way up.

For believe me: the secret for harvesting from existence the greatest fruitfulness and greatest enjoyment is – to live dangerously.

Friedrich Nietzsche

12 SURPRISE

Bob was a kid like an alternating current at school. He was in school, he was out of school, he was in, he was out. When he wasn't suspended, expelled or in some kind of programme, he strutted around school like a Roman statue bristling with evil. Bob was medicated just to tone him down to bristling evil level. He was tall and athletic, extremely strong and well developed for his age, chiselled, hairy, and with this demonic energy that made him dangerous to be around. Even his hair was tightly curled by this energy, and his eyes were fierce and burning.

Bob was a genuine legend. The first person I ever met with the true power of miracles about him. He came from European aristocracy on one side of his family, money on the other. He not only had an aeroplane in his household but had already crashed it in a jungle. A souvenir photograph existed, one I didn't see until much later, one he didn't boast about. It was taken from above by a helicopter; and there he stood in linen trousers and a gold-buttoned blazer on the fractured wings of this plane, glaring up.

By the time he was my friend we were of driving age. Danger grew exponentially. He was soon a man who would throw a car door open in traffic to confront someone who had looked at him the wrong way. He'd not only dare them to get out and be assassinated but would lean through the window to any female companion and tell her to leave the loser and come with him. It was ridiculous. I've seen him standing like Atlas with his hands on his hips in three lanes of crawling traffic daring cars full of men to get out, and that in a country full of guns.

No one ever heard of him being challenged. He just had the equation. There are fearsome-looking men and there are crazy-looking men, but he was fearsome and crazy. The equation was in his eyes: he would stop at nothing, any time. He didn't pick his battles: this one right here will do fine, and if there isn't one let's have one. It meant there was a curve to knowing him, there was maths involved, because early in high school we were uniformly wary of him, if not afraid. But like all great sources of energy he both repelled and attracted, and the mathematical curve over the course of years either expelled you out of orbit or brought you slowly in. There was a big spike the day he stalked and beat up one of our teachers for being rude to him, at last bell in front of the whole school. Then for obvious reasons he wasn't in school any more, but he was soon driving, and came to haunt the street outside.

That's when our friendship was sealed. We were a bit more civilised by then, and we were in that late teenhood where we *considered* ourselves civilised. In practical terms it meant Bob was now tolerable half of the time; the other half you had to watch out. He was still prone to fits of abandoned energy, when he felt compelled to piss where he stood, or scale large public structures.

One day I was eating *ceviche* in a street restaurant with another friend when Bob drove by, saw us, and came in. He was wild that day. I invited him to sit with us but he insisted on standing and flailing and bleating in our faces. I tried to quieten him down, it was a regular place full of people who didn't have to suffer our excesses over their food. But Bob just got louder. He was electric. There was no settling him down.

In the end I stood up and punched him. A solid thump in the shoulder.

I waited for a flood of blows. The whole restaurant waited.

Seafood stood still. Music seemed to stop.

But as the shock subsided, Bob's face simply fell. He stared at me.

Then his lip curled, and he strode out across the street to the opposite corner, where he stood with his back to us.

It was a surprise. I went to him and paced around like a repentant lover, reasoning to his back. He kept spinning away, tragic and crestfallen. It wasn't the scene of a man so offended that he stormed away for ever, it was the pathetic scene of a boy standing in deliberate view of us, it was an invitation to woo him back.

SCENE B

One evening after the punch had been forgotten, Bob called me to say he'd committed suicide. He was at home, his parents were away. Enough was enough, this vale of tears, etcetera, and goodbye. I said, 'I'll be right over,' because he sounded alive still. As I put the phone down, the other corner of our triangle, Tony, rang to tell me that Bob had just called to say he'd committed suicide. He sounded alive enough to him too, and we agreed to meet at the nearest intersection and fly in a convoy to Bob's house. It was a genuine licence and we used it to the limit, racing those few miles through town like ambulance men. It wasn't the kind of place or time, and Bob wasn't the type of guy, to call an ambulance to. It never crossed our minds. In the parallel language of our trio the calls meant you guys come alone. We were the ambulance.

At his place we found the doors conveniently ajar, specifically those that led to the death scene; but it was a big enough house that when we took a wrong turn into the living room he called out, 'In here!' before resuming a deathly moan.

We found him in a bathroom behind the kitchen, in the tub, smeared with blood. He'd cut his wrists across, not deep enough to die, but messy.

Once we were satisfied that he wasn't still bleeding, we hauled him out, dangling like a kitten, and asked what could possibly make him do it.

'You forgot my birthday,' he said.

'Bob,' we said. 'Your fucking birthday is tomorrow.'

Here's where writing resembles life: Bob's character setup at the top of the chapter gives a fair idea of how I saw him, if not how he was, in the days when I first knew him. Anyone who was there would probably recognise him from that description, even without the name. Something like that setup is what many new writers would use to establish a character in a novel. And what a great character he would make, the new original cat among pigeons. Except that in the setup he's one-dimensional. We see how he looks, we hear how he behaves, but we don't see who he *is*. In life the two vulnerable moments he showed me were him. They're what stayed with me. Suddenly the legend was human, those glimpses shifted the paradigm and exposed him for who he was underneath the behaviour. At a stroke they explained and forgave it. In our early days at school we all perceived him one-dimensionally, it's all we could do. He projected himself one-dimensionally. Those of us who never let a perverse fascination draw us in will still think that's all there was to him; because that's how we are, there are too many people around to discover all their natures. But my bond only grew after those moments. I suddenly knew I had to look after *him* – which is a hell of a shift from the character I set up. Crazy Bob, whose entire persona was built around kicking ass, needed the most looking after. He was a child.

As in life, those scenes have to happen in writing. We bond with our characters when their windows open, when we see things they don't know they're showing us, or, better still, things they don't want to show us, things their whole persona is designed to hide. Only vulnerable villains have real motivations.

Apart from the illumination and bonding this brings, even to unpleasant characters, there's something else in it for writing which should be a watchword, especially if you want pages to turn: surprise. Revelations like these are energy pills in a narrative, pivots on which a story swings in new directions. The two plot-points in a novel, between beginning and middle, and middle and end, often need no more than revelations like these – because surprise combined with new insight shifts the story to a deeper level. In a novel where Bob was protagonist, the first plot-point would be one of the scenes above. He starts the novel as a madman, piles shit around himself, is painted a soulless rogue – then we see the truth. He goes from strength to weakness in a blow. In the middle we would explore that weakness, things would go badly for him, his chickens would come home to roost, chapter by chapter. But at the second plot-point, changed by admitting his weakness, he would have to discover new strength. Just when all seemed lost, he would have to grow up.

Whenever we hit a point in fiction where something has to happen – even just a phone ringing, or someone showing up – it serves us well to ask what could be the most surprising thing to happen, within the scope of the story, in the same way we ask what the worst obstruction could be to our protagonist's goals. Not only does someone catch him in bed with the teacher, it's the teacher's partner who bursts in. You'll find that fiction is tolerant of big news. The modern day is extremely tolerant of it. There's a muting effect to written fiction, which is fine when it's about the nightingale singing up the sun; but in the drama of a scene between people, especially where there's high conflict, it's hard to go too far. What's the worst thing, and what's the most surprising thing – ask yourself whenever a door opens.

Writing people is one of the pleasures of the job, characters can surprise you before you know what you've written. Just keep pushing them out of their comfort zone to see who they really are. What would the scene be like where Bob went to apply for an office job? Where he fathered a handicapped child, ran for political office?

He eventually made up on the street corner in front of the *ceviche* joint. I used every plea in the book and he finally came around. The restaurant, open to the street, all but applauded us as we made our way back through the traffic. Bob still needled me accusingly for a while afterwards. But it was soon enough forgotten.

Likewise, in five minutes we brought him back from his suicide.

All it took both times with fearsome Bob was a hug.

What once were vices are manners now.

Seneca

13 WATER BALLOON

In a logical sense addiction is only a problem when you can't get your drug. But an issue with certain drugs is that they're costly. With expensive drugs, be they women, men, shopping, casinos or cocaine, it can happen that their financial drain sets up a vicious circle: you dampen your alarm with the drug but as the drain grows you get more alarmed and need more drug, which causes more alarm.

The only time I ever hit the wall with a drug, once I just couldn't buy any more, I soon felt cured of it. By definition I was suddenly clean, which is what we're supposed to be. Costs fell to zero, which meant that any cash could go towards what it was supposed to, which was clearing debt. I didn't have a fraction of what that required; but I had devised a betting system for horses that showed real promise, a counterintuitive tricasting system that went against favourites. I began to use that to parlay small change into cash. By now you can see where this is headed.

I couldn't see where it was headed. Welcome to the wonderful world of the water-balloon model: squeeze the fucker one end and it pops out the other. I'll abbreviate the rest of the story to the point where I finally figured things out: after years clinging to the popular model that says when we conquer our demons they just go away, and even after thinking that I'd conquered mine, I had occasion, painfully, over years, to watch someone I knew, a beautiful soul, being squeezed from insecurity to anorexia to bulimia to agoraphobia to anxiety to alcoholism to suicidal depression and probably self-harm. I saw it closely enough to know that there was no shifting that demon by any means; squeeze it here, it popped out there. And I saw that, in large part, those disorders were spoken of and treated as a host of separate demons, with separate specialists and theories and treatments. But I could see that they were only the blisters of a single rampant mass, one that had its own intelligence, at least to the extent that it decided to destroy its host and nothing else.

Take a balloon, half fill it with water and squeeze it in your hand to see it bulge this way and that, refusing to be captured or diminished. This is my guess at the model governing demons and other energy-dependent phenomena that we try to control, as with government crack-downs, economic policies, social change. You don't diminish the mass, you merely shift it: crack down on porn, sex crimes go up; crack down on drugs, booze gets a boost. So what I'd unknowingly done over a period of years was transfer one demonic mass through a series of manifestations, passing it down a line like a rugby ball, still thinking of each pass as an issue conquered. In the end I was lucky, a good mind drew my attention to the mass and I started making my own discoveries. Over time the demon grew half-hearted and I converted it back to sport for a while, becoming a fitness fascist. After that I made valves to feed the thing in small doses and stop it from plotting to destroy anything; finally it made a home on the written page where I can joust with it and write it into reason. The point is that the most realistic outcome of trying to kill an unwanted mass is its transference to something else. They're an energy that can be converted but not destroyed, short of life-bombing medication. Insecurity into religion, anger into sport, sedatives into wanking, eating into shopping.

Such homespun truths might seem obvious but maybe they can give us an edge in writing characters. Whether they're in jail or outer space you don't often see the mass identified and exposed behind a goal or weakness; yet our stories through the ages are full of such conversions, from good to bad, upright to fallen, despair to 'seeing the light'.

The notion that the chimerae on our backs can't be destroyed and have their own intelligence, are their own antagonists and protagonists, shifting and repolarising behind ideas, can give characters a dynamic core that keeps them moving inside and out. Given that we live in the age of the headfuck I feel there's mileage in it for modern writing, or at least for observing the behaviour around us.

The maxim: headfucks have a mothership.

We don't lose it, we move it.

All God's children are not beautiful. Most of God's children are, in fact, barely presentable.

Fran Lebowitz

14 PRESSURE-COOKER

When I was small I sailed on a liner across the Pacific and Atlantic oceans via the Panama Canal. It took weeks but that was fine, it was a serious ship built for going places and not a barge-hotel for fucking around in shallows waiting for Tiki-doll vendors in canoes, although I did get a Tiki doll on shore so it wasn't about them as such. The ship had two funnels and made good speed so that if you struggled to the point of the bow against the wind and poised yourself facing back, it would blast you down the deck like a cannonball. Between this and dropping safety pins on a thread into the sea in the hope of catching flying fish, I had a life and was busy with it.

Outside was tacky with salt, inside smelled of gravy. Somewhere lower down there was a place that smelled of finger-paint and glue which was the children's area. King Neptune Club, my arse. It was dressed up as a club but you could see it was a small detention centre. Flowing from the then-still-fairly-recent institution of childhood it seemed that zealous adults had clumsily taken it upon themselves to manufacture a whole set of parameters governing comfort zones for children. These included imagining that we preferred the company of fellow cannibals, and that we thrived on supervision by implausible wide-eyed zealots who sometimes fucking sang.

I went to this 'club' one day and faced these sinister

grinners. There was no singing at least, it was time to paint and draw – and it so happened that I could draw pretty well for my age, by a probably reliable consensus not including family.

I spent that afternoon with my tongue out concentrating on some picture. I think it featured horses. During that serene time I developed a nodding relationship with fellow prisoners. An older boy even came to look at my drawing; then he silently went away. After a while I watched him on his way back, pulling a stern-looking grinner along with him. The boy pointed me out from a distance. Pointing is never a good sign when you're young. The pair came and gathered around my drawing.

'This boy says the drawing's his,' said the grinner.

'Eh? What?'

The man frowned and put it to me that it was bad form to steal someone else's artwork and present it as my own. The worst kind of form. I should be expelled from the club and eke the rest of my days out in shame. This was the gist of it. If attitude had been fashionable I could've said, 'And what the fuck do you think I've been doing all day with my tongue out?' But attitude was unfashionable back in the day. Not only unfashionable it was bad, touted as the first step towards mayhem and social collapse. A spankable offence. You had to suck things up.

I protested and laid on some drama but Grinner's mind was made up. 'Because look,' he said. 'This is a good drawing. He's a bigger boy, which one of you could possibly do such a drawing? Obviously the bigger boy.'

He made me drink the whole quart and apologise, then

publicly expelled me from the glue-borstal. I couldn't believe it. The paradigm just swung away and never came back. And once the paradigm swings, any further protest makes you a bigger dick, this is what I learned at sea. I can't tie a sailor's knot or navigate by the stars, but I can tell you that once a situation repolarises, you just have to wait it out. Even so, the experience flowed into something pertinent to writing: I was stuck in a crucible. We were still at sea for weeks after the supposed art heist, and there was nowhere to run. Day after day, on the decks, at breakfast, at dinner, the antagonist and other contagonist types were all around. I couldn't escape them. If the conflict had continued, the ship would have been a pressure-cooker – just as it should be in writing. If conflict is central to characters' passages through a novel, it works best when the parties can't escape each other. In *Vernon God Little* the cooker was the town of Martirio, and within that the peeling wood house where Vernon lived. It worked because he was stuck there. It means that our story about the vicious divorce can't just have characters bickering on the phone; they need to be snowed in together in a cabin, house-bound caring for someone else, working in the same building – or stuck on a ship at sea.

When we ignite passions in a sealed arena we arm explosions. If books are about humans being tested it makes sense to cook them together.

The ship was an inspired setting for my art scandal, it would have made a great cooker if I hadn't had to suck things up and get over them. Typical scene my trickster mentor-deity writes for me, barely seven years old and already involved in art scandals. What I took from it, after noting that balls and reputation alone were enough to pass off bullshit, was the taste of confinement with a lit fuse. Antagonists didn't even have to show up; tension grew from simply knowing that they could.

My response at the time was to hang out with grown-ups. They could be trusted never to claim anything of mine as theirs. Within that milieu, aided by a favourite aunt of the 'why not?' variety, I pursued adult pastimes that soon led to jackpot bingo in the evenings. I honed my taste for chance with it and within days won the jackpot, thirty-five bucks, a fortune, back when seven years old was seven years old.

As if crucibles respected karma and delivered ironic morals.

In this case: that art just doesn't pay.

At least half the mystery novels published violate the law that the solution, once revealed, must seem to be inevitable.

Raymond Chandler

15 DÉNOUEMENT

We moved house when I was ten. It was to my last family home, the only one I would call home in the end, a modernist slab of two and a half concrete and glass storeys built amid lava flows from an old volcanic eruption in the south of Mexico City. To me it was a James Bond villain's headquarters. You could see the city's guardian volcanoes from the balconies, and a shorter distance behind us climbed a range to almost thirteen thousand feet where Xitle's crater had spewed the black ground I lived on. Those hills later became a stomping ground whose scents of pine and oak bathed my first romance; but first came time to stomp at the house, a place of darting lizards, songbirds, possums and the nocturnal cries of the peacocks next door, a *Tarzan* soundtrack that can still infect dreams today. The grounds were landscaped with jungles and rockeries that swirled with such drama around the flow of the lava that imagination was redundant for play. Between these gardens and the building's guest apartments, its storerooms, steam room and boiler room, I carved out a domain.

The previous owner didn't empty the house completely. He left a polar-bear rug with head and paws, a hundred or more copies of a journal on breeding Californian rabbits – which, as an accomplished brochure-thief, fed my obsession with printed materials – and a gardener called

José, who was also gatekeeper and lived in a little house by the gates. We brought some staff from our old house, including a cook, a housekeeper and a maid, who all disliked each other but who could be made to laugh together by the right antics. The cook laughed like a drain, the maid tittered and the housekeeper laughed in spite of herself. They obviously kept secrets for each other, but only as grudgingly as the Soviet Union and the USA left missiles unlaunched. Their apartments were in a separate storey on top of the house which also housed the laundry. They reached it by paths and steps through a lava garden, and it was *terra incognita* to me, apart from an occasional mission to find the dog, who became attached to the laundry lady and knew the times she came.

The subject of this story, though, is José. He must have been in his mid-twenties, a gentle presence in a slept-in white T-shirt who could frown with attention without losing his smile, who sharpened his own mower blades and was able to build and repair things in his workshop. One day, I played a gag and came by with a plastic building nail that fitted onto a finger to look as if it had gone through. There was blood painted on it. José recoiled, flew for some pliers and told me to brace myself; then sagged when I showed him the trick. He should've nailed me to the workbench, but he laughed.

This easy-listening idyll of values never so safe again, this *Bewitched* meets Pérez Prado for cocktails, of occasional houseguests called Bob and Frank and Elmer whose sports coats were chequered and whose whiskey had ginger and ice, chuckling 'goddamit' and 'hell' or, if I was around, 'heck'; this place of ambassadors and Weight-Watchers, of positive thinking and Juicy Fruit gum, Erica Jong and varicose veins – was stopped in its tracks one day, because José disappeared. Just like that. The maid, who was probably closest to his age, came with me to find out if he had really gone. I went into the gatehouse and it was bare, left neatly empty of his stuff. It was a mystery. My parents couldn't work it out. I couldn't even work it out, and by then I was in a special relationship with certain staff where we turned blind eyes to each other's skulduggery. Their skulduggery was more important than mine, it involved inflating household shopping lists and passing bags of extras through the gates at night to young men who whisked them to dusty outskirts where roosters replaced peacocks and life made our place an obscenity. It was a controlled leak, a small, reliable and vital one, and noble in execution, it wasn't a slippery slope. My family could travel for months, leaving the house to staff alone, and return to find everything in its place and all accounts in order.

My skulduggery had to do with escape, with scurrying out like a rat onto the streets, roaming and tasting *pulque* with workmen next door who were building a wall of lava rock carved to fit like a puzzle without concrete or mortar.

Later on the girls helped by filtering drugs from my laundry.

Even with such a relationship there were no clues about José. Everyone was sorry, and it was a shame because he had been there for years and had considered the place his home. My parents were good employers, they paid well, gave gifts and accommodated problems. So who knows? The next gardener was Selerino. He could speak Mixtec, a pre-Columbian language which he shyly taught me some words in. Then the travelling season was upon us and by the time we got back he'd gone too.

It was a blight. In the abbreviated seasons of that life, a revolving Aztec calendar of home and abroad, yet another gardener came and went, and soon after that the maid came shuffling in tears to meet with my parents. She had grown plump and confessed that she was going to have a baby. She had been afraid my folks would let her go, but she hadn't got that idea from them. What's more my mother loved babies and made special provision for that one, bought all his stuff and cooed and made him smile when he arrived; but he died in infancy of an illness that came with him.

Thunderous waves even roll through places designed to shut thundering out. Because we were just people on a boat like any other, stuck with each other, dependent, connected like deck hands in a routine. We'd lost three men overboard, and now a little life mocked the round-the-clock thump of easy jazz from the stereo in the hall. The calendar kept revolving, the volcanoes kept their snow, first romance grew a scent of forests in the hills – and another gardener passed through.

Finally, I was the last of the family in the house. My father was ill in New York, my mother was with him, and the peacocks cried only for me. One day, even the staff were out. I went looking for scissors and ventured up to the laundry, where I heard noises from the apartments. Someone was there, in the maid's rooms. I knocked, and finally looked inside – and it was a young girl minding a toddler.

Gardeners' children. They lived a twilight life on the roof, without school, without escape as long as we were there, invisible for years. Gardeners had just fled.

The older child would be José's.

The memory explodes with implications, not least what the maid must have felt over the years. Sure, the one tragic baby we knew of was a fair clue; but the timing didn't match any other mysterious rhythms around the house, not the gardener rhythm anyway. The memory is here because without any devices of plotting it has the natural framework of a mystery, keeping all its secrets till the end. The clues are under our noses but the answers don't come till seasons later, lighting up in a retrospective chain. As with most stories the subjects and circumstances are nominal and interchangeable, only the dynamic stays the same. So it's the same structure as the mystery where at the back of the fridge you find the wallet you were looking for three months ago; only then do you remember the party that night.

What's happening in this model is that the answer to the mystery is improbable from the point at which we ask the question, which is the beginning; we don't say, 'There goes another gardener, the roof must be full of kids'; or 'My wallet's missing, I'll check the fridge.' From question to answer the clues are unconnected, out of sight. The thing is like a ferry chain across a river; we see a chain on our bank before it disappears into the water. That's the end of its story if the ferry isn't there, and we don't find the chain on the other side. Mystery.

In writing, the art lies in showing just enough chain, the flash of links here and there to make a plausible continuum when we look back from the end. The chain is one of possibility, each link explaining the next; but until we see them linked there's only black water. For instance, it seems impossible that someone could live in our house for years unbeknownst to us, or even be born to someone we knew without us noticing. The keys to it happening lie in the seasons of travel and the scale of the house. Without them it couldn't have happened. In this tale they happened for real, but they would also be plausible in writing; because the links we see at the beginning – the setting and the travel – explain them. The clues are there. The setting is big and the staff has its quarters away from the main house – *terra incognita*. The family travelled a lot and the maid lucked out – or didn't – because her first and last pregnancies, at least their most visible phases, coincided with our absence for weeks or months. Combine that with her annual leave, or with a period of sick leave that I remember her taking, and she could have had four straight months to herself. Plus it's harder to notice someone changing when you see them daily, the change creeps up on you. Unless you have physical contact, clues can be disguised.

If we were to add more clues in writing, they might be unexplained noises from the roof at night, some *frisson* between maid and gardeners, some near-miss visits to the laundry. As it stands this slice of life is a chain's head and tail already writhing. At one end, the move to a new house where a character lives; then a plot-point – the character disappears without trace; and a dénouement – his kid is upstairs and we deduce that he fled before her birth. If it were to be a novel it would need a protagonist with a burning goal – the gardener's brother trying to find him, the gardener himself heir to a fortune which his kin come to fight over, unaware of a new heir upstairs; or simply an observer whose passion was to solve the gardener mysteries. It played out in my life as a subplot, more relevant to José and the maid than to me directly. Neither could narrate the story because they know too much, but the maid could be an antagonist, a gardener-eater who obstructs investigations; or another staff member could antagonise by blackmailing the maid over what they knew. My role as contagonist, aiding the deception by trading blind eyes, would be the same in the novel as in life.

Bang. Art imitates life imitating art.

One practical key to plotting like this is to use the writer's advantage: unlike nature we're not confined to forward motion. If the brain scrambles wondering how a chain will link from implausible to plausible, plot the thing backwards. Imagine the most impossible outcome, then plant clues before it. See how many mysteries put their ending first: a man is found hanging from the hands of Big Ben. How did he get there? That's the rest of the story.

One thing the technique gives in spades: compelling first lines, first paragraphs and first chapters.

'On Sunday I found children living at my place who I'd never seen before.'

The universe is made of stories, not of atoms.

Muriel Rukeyser

16 REVERSE *TITANIC*

We used to score weed from a doctor.

See the image that conjures.

For a while after I left my childhood home I occupied a beautifully crumbling three-storey building down an alley in the old heart of Mexico City. Not chic crumbling, with awnings and cappuccinos nearby, but real crumbling. Still, all crumbling is to an extent chic, and the building had dusty floor-to-ceiling French windows and questionable little balconies, and one of its toilets worked if you used a bucket to flush it. Across the street a heavily guarded nightclub full of guns, bad suits and Brylcreem spat light and voices up the alley at night. By contrast, on the corner in the mornings a man blended fresh juices of orange, pineapple, papaya, oatmeal, beetroot and raw egg, which cured everything. And in this neighbourhood lived an old man called Fernando, in his eighties but unfettered by it. Fernando sometimes had the best weed, kilos of it, in the form of whole dried plants wrapped in newsprint. Other times he didn't have it, but thought that he might get some in weeks to come.

Over time we gathered that he was a medical doctor. He didn't live in a better building than I did, and was of a generation that regarded crumbling as crumbling and not cool. And it turned out that he'd been struck off the medical register for practising abortions before they became legal anywhere in Mexico. It had been some time before, but Fernando kept practising them, safely, against a national backdrop where a fifth of all maternal mortalities were due to unsafe abortions among the poor. And some of those poor, in states like Oaxaca and Michoacán, hadn't the means to pay for his services. But they could get their hands on plenty of good weed.

We little shits used to buy it from him. One of us went on to write this little story, which if it made any money, and some were sent to the poor in Oaxaca and Michoacán, would complete a cycle. But that's tempting Fate.

None of this is to weigh into arguments on abortion, but rather to see how the statement 'We used to score weed from a doctor' grew a tail; and how it ended up being the meatiest part of the story, a tail made of steps in a life, coiling back into darkness. Because presumably Fernando was a bright kid in the early twentieth century. Presumably he entered medicine with a zesty religion for healing, went on to form moral judgements about the situations around him. He must have known the glow of achievement and respect among peers. He must have known power, and lived well. If you wrote the novel, where would you start the narrative? Would it be with a serious, bespectacled teen seeing injustice in the Mexican revolution, making pacts with himself for the future? Would it be a young woman in a makeshift hut on a hillside, freshly scrubbed, dressed and smelling of lavender water, watching her mother at the door scan the night for a stranger's arrival with a medicine bag, like an exorcist? Would it be we rakes across the road from the nightclub, completing the cycle of service, unaware of the pain and the lavender water?

Nothing is ever just, 'We used to score weed from a doctor.' Even if we only write that much we should take into account every statement's tail in a story, and let some of it unfold as a subplot to give lifelike depth to a piece. Looking at the way things seem to work in life, it's unusual that a single purposeful action leads to a defined result later on. But that's the way we package it in retrospect – 'He took out his last hundred dollars and sunk it into a kitchen-table start-up called Microsoft.' Not one but ten circumstances doomed the *Titanic*. The more you watch how things unfold, the more you see the *Titanic* effect in operation: not one but many events lining up to deliver an apparently fateful outcome, which is the romantic or memorable or tragic result we condense the whole story into, making it a badge. I wanted to look at this because if we start to observe it in life and understand its feel, we should build that kind of reality into our plots. Imagine the domino effect when, out of a rotating lottery of possibilities between characters and settings, we get to see the wrong ones line up one by one.

It sounds like a strategic nightmare to pull off, but it's as easy to set up in a book as it is to watch in life. Once you have the beginnings of a plot, and one subplot beneath it, you'll find that they intersect and suggest other subplots, which will also intersect throughout a story: a man goes to the bank, his wife at home gets a call from a friend in trouble, the bank manager is in personal strife; these are all separate stories, but they want to play with each other like dolphins in the bow-wave of a narrative, intersecting when our character arrives at the bank. So at the beginning of a scene, when asking how best to obstruct the character in his goal, or what the biggest surprise could be, the answer lies in these subplots. This is the way books grow, and how you end up with a multitude of existing triggers for a *Titanic* effect that resembles life. It's not enough to put new twists into a book as they occur to you – they have to flow naturally from the threads that are there. In practice this often means going back to earlier sections and plumbing new threads in to support a new twist; as they say, if a gun gets fired in the last chapter, we need to know it's in a drawer in the first. Intersections can be as surprising as you like: the wife's friend in trouble turns out to be the bank manager's wife, our character's wife loans her money, the troubled bank manager hears about it just before our man enters to ask for a loan, and in a gust of relief, grants the loan – or the reverse. Bang, bang, bang, bang, bang.

In the following scene from *Lights Out in Wonderland*, the protagonist Gabriel Brockwell urgently needs a decadent party to help a friend out of trouble. He's found the right venue, but it's occupied by humble non-partygoers – or so he thinks. Scenes like this where characters come together are power-pills in a narrative, crossroads like the coffee shop or bar in every sitcom where information is exchanged and delusions meet hard reality. I mark the subplots here as they can be hard to isolate in a moving narrative, which is just as it should be. But if you separate the interactions in a scene you'll see that once a narrative is in flight each scene is a composite of subplots travelling alongside each other, intersecting at moments like this to drive the story forward. Meanwhile, in dialogue we set up tension for future scenes, explain past histories, and unload information between players.

⋘◉⋙

Main narrative: Gabriel sets off on a crucial mission and is immediately thwarted:

Bile rattles up my throat. I decide to chance crossing the foyer to the lavatories. But with my first step Gisela's voice turns especially caustic, and I shrink back to the wall:

Subplot one: two secondary characters continue a bitter argument, one originally sparked by Gabriel's appearance in town. While he cliff-hangs waiting to move, we overhear past histories that feed the deeper narrative, and also add clues and flesh to other subplots, such as that of ex-Stasi agent Gottfried Pietsch:

'Oh ja,' she spits, 'so romantic, with Gottfried on the Baltic. For old times' sake we even bring our own *Stasi* agent to monitor us.'

'*Gott*, Gisela, *shhh* – he's having a bad time. It's not like he'll be in our room, we're just giving him a ride to the place. You know he'll spend the whole day in a *strandkorb* with some brandy and a hunting magazine. This break was meant to cheer you up.'

'And see me grinning like a honey-cake horse.'

A whine works its way into Gerd's voice: 'I'm very sorry it's not the night at the *kino* you wanted for your life. Still, you seem to have survived. Life's not over. The *kino*'s still there, we can still try. I worked hard to see you had all you needed. Life's not a dream, Gisela! Times are hard for the working man!'

'Oh the big working man, with his investment Wurst. Fifteen years I spent heating Würstchen and washing cups, and now that it's finished I have nothing. You have nothing. Not even the toaster, the oven or the cups.'

'We have a coffee machine. They're not cheap.'

'My father bought the machine! Gerd!'

'But you're not blaming me? Business is a risk. That's how business is. A risk! Do you think I planned for us to get nothing? Is it my fault they close the airport? It could have been the other way – perhaps Berlin decides this is the greatest airport, and fills it with planes until we're rich. Then what? You'd be every night at the *kino*!'

'Are you blind now as well? Look at the place! It's a tomb! Do people get rich in a tomb? Or do they get buried there?!'

'Bah, come on.'

'Come on? Come on! I took my risk too! I could have been out of here! You wish the wall was still standing so you could hide behind it in the East! Where you wouldn't have to get anywhere in life! You and Gottfried and all your grey cronies could've just stayed there hissing about every-one else without having to prove yourselves any better!'

'Don't start with old times again.'

'Old times? *These* are my old times! *These* ones! *They* were *new* times, and I was on my way out of this place like a bird!'

'Bah,' Gerd's face falls in the tone of his voice: 'Well, why didn't you just go then?'

'I should have done!'

'You should have just gone then. Why blame me years later for something you should have done, I can't do it for you.'

'Because *I felt sorry for you!*'

Whoosh. Silence follows in shockwaves.

In the pause between this and the sound of cheap heels, Gerd's eyes appear in my mind, perched on the edge of their sockets. 'Where are you going?' he calls after her. 'What about the trip? Should I just cancel it?'

'Do what you want!' Gisela clacks out of the kiosk. I hold my breath as she passes. The Mercedes is still outside, but so fearsome is Gisela's energy, such is the friction of her entry into the earth's gravitational field, that it pulls away before she can sear any paintwork. The figures in the back don't stir. I watch the car turn onto Columbiadamm, a donkey's ear of steam poking from the exhaust.

With all that on board, Gabriel can finally move forward:

With these departures a weight lifts off me. After some deep breaths, tuning my ear for sounds of Gerd, I set off across the foyer. In the terminal only a few moving forms mill about; older sorts waiting for something that mightn't come. I descend the few steps, glancing around. The lavatories are down some more stairs to my right, but as I turn for them something hot trickles to my lip.

I touch it, and it's blood.

Stopping to dab my nose, I see a small figure cross the concourse. I only notice because it cocks its head in that questioning way of parrots and dogs. While I try to lick blood from my face, or wipe it onto my hand and lick that instead, the form moves into focusing range. It's a young woman in a red coat and beret. She lowers a mobile phone from her ear, and pockets it.

It's Anna from the kiosk.

Subplot two: a romantic interest appears. Her subplot grows through encounters like this to eventually pay off at the climax. In the meantime, of course, Gabriel is thwarted again, and his chances with her look hopeless:

I go to draw my overcoat around me but find my fly broken open, my underwear missing, and my belt still undone. A lump of sick heaves into my mouth. When I try to swallow it, my nose starts to pour like a tap. I spit the lump and hold an open sleeve under my nose, pretending to fuss with my hair, moving strands with a finger.

Anna slows a few paces away, expressionless, finally stopping to look me up and down. 'You missed a hair,' she eventually points.

I lower my sleeve. Blood pours onto my foot.

'Do you need an ambulance?'

Before answering I suck a wad back up my nose. It crackles well enough, but blood still splats to the floor, and runs to my mouth. One drop hangs off my lip for a moment before falling. 'I think I just need some cakes,' I croak.

She nods slowly: 'To eat – or to put up your nose?'

Now adrenaline calls drugs back to life. I start lightly tripping, and end up absorbed in the spatterings on the floor. She stands staring till I begin to sway.

'Is that a normal Thursday night for you?' she asks.

'Pretty much. Though sometimes I go out for a drink.'

I detect a minuscule rising of eyebrows. Not mirth. But not not mirth. And she says: 'Gerd might have a cake for you. Can you find the bathroom?'

'Yes, thank you. Thanks, Anna, for that.'

'Pff,' she turns away, coat bobbing daintily like a bell.

The narrative moves on as Gabriel (aka Frederick) continues his mission:

I stumble to the conveniences. They sit clean and empty in their underground domain, a cool oasis where you and I can regroup. The splash of my emptying body decks them with echoes – forgive me for that – then cold water staunches blood loss, and more or less cleans up my face. I sit for a while on a toilet, spinning, until the lack of cakes becomes an emergency. Gerd isn't familiar with me day-to-day, I reason, so he mightn't think my state unusual. He needn't see me barefoot, if he's inside the kiosk and I approach along the wall. I button my coat to its full length and make my way upstairs.

'Frederick,' he smiles through the glass – then: '*Mein Gott* – what happened? Where are your shoes? Come, come, sit down.'

'I just need some cakes.'

'*Haa* – already training for our little party? It might be a wild night tonight, eh? But you're about twelve hours too early.'

The scene ends with the promise of a party, which is what Gabriel wanted from the start. But it also hooks us into the next scene: can it really be the kind of high-flying party he needs? Between the hook of entering the building under pressure, to the hook of an impending party, we've taken a detour through the lives and times of four characters, fleshing out the past as well as portending a troublesome future. More importantly for the main narrative, we've increased the protagonist's hopelessness. That's what the job of subplotting is about; it's why on page one we don't just say, 'There's going to be a party.'

This dissection shows the scene from the writer's side of the fence. It seems contrived to stop Gabriel's mission to overhear someone fight, then stop it again to bump into a girl; but that's what we have to do, only making sure that circumstances arise naturally. Intersections like this are particularly vital for first-person voices: when the narrator is a character, we're confined in our viewpoint to what he can personally see and hear, and so have to be creative to keep him informed. For all that twisting and turning, these constructions still pass unnoticed to someone reading the book. Each subplot, then, is part of the event-cascade moving through intersections towards a *Titanic* effect at the climax. It might seem a tangle of plumbing when you lift the hatch on an isolated scene like this, but it all started by putting four people into a book and letting them grow and collide. It resembles life: the society we're in and the state of our times is not a result of forward thinking but of serial opportunism; someone discovered that greed and vanity drive sales and only then turned them into bigger plans. Likewise, we're opportunists when we play God with characters in a book – watch them, see what's possible, then build it into their lives. If you write a setting with characters at a table, you'll soon see which is the likely or unlikely villain, and away the story goes.

The *Titanic* effect also comes to bear on the act of writing, or rather the reverse *Titanic* effect, because we want a number of not necessarily bad conditions to gather

– something to say, and something to urge or excite us; enough force to dive in and start; the commitment to see it through, to scale past twenty, fifty, a hundred pages; and we want the calm and earnest resignation of the watchmaker to sift through it all again and again and tighten it up till it crackles.

In the case of my first novel, all these conditions came about. It didn't make anything easy, take note – but possible. As for Fernando the old doctor, until one of us writes the whole story, these are the potential subplots we have: the crumbling building, the nightclub, the abortion patients, the weed buyers and the juice man on the corner. It's enough. Once we got going, those steps would sprout other steps, of his wives, his lovers, his patients, and all the links flying off them to infinity, a writhing mass of possibilities.

Our job is to isolate and tie pertinent ones together into a coherent story, allowing glimpses of the lives behind them.

That house in the alley near Fernando's place, across the street from the nightclub where you sensed everyone was called Pablo or Lola, was let to me by a mentor and friend, a fine artist who lived eight blocks away and who woke up one morning with a view over the city after an earthquake shook down a wall of his building. He took it as a hint and moved his family to an island in the Caribbean, just before a landmark hurricane swept through. Where would you start that novel?

'We used to score weed from a doctor.'

The best part of the fiction in many novels is the notice that the characters are purely imaginary.

Franklin P. Adams

17 IMMUNE RESPONSE

Listen to a table full of holidaymakers:

'Shall we try the sausage place for dinner?'

'Mmm, I've been disappointed by the sausage place. The chops last time weren't great. But I saw an awesome-looking Polynesian around the corner.'

'I had the chops last time and they were excellent.'

'Yeah, problem is I've had really Michelin-star chops before, I know how they should be. Not the way the sausage place does them.'

'Bet they cost more than six euros.'

'What do Polynesians eat anyway?'

'Kind of Pacific Rim, I guess, Asian fusion type of thing. Place looks awesome, you could smell it across the road.'

'Well, I'm easy, you guys decide. The only thing I'm NOT having is any more rice. Why are they so addicted to rice with everything?'

'I think Polynesians like their rice.'

'Eh? Forget it, then.'

'Come on – it's bound to be a varied cuisine, don't just boil it down to rice. The place looks great, full of people. Smells were incredible.'

'Why don't we do the sausage place and you just order something else? It's a bit harsh to judge them on one dish, they had a varied menu too.'

'No, listen, I'm quite happy to do the sausage place again. Whatever anyone wants. You can all eat, and I'll grab a sandwich when I get back to the room.'

'For God's sake.'

'I'm telling you there's an awesome Polynesian around the bloody corner. I've had Polynesian before and it was amazing.'

'You never said you'd had it before. Did he?'

'I've never been with you for Polynesian! When did you go?'

'Work thing, you know.'

'Well, you never told me about it if it's so awesome.'

'Barry's retirement party, probably was.'

'Shh, everyone: a compromise – Chinese?'

'We can do that at home.'

'Rice! No way.'

'Well, if Polynesian is Asian fusion it can't be a million miles away!'

'Rice coming out of me bloody ears.'

'Looks like tapas again, then.'

'I could do tapas, actually.'

'Again? Well, I'm easy. You go ahead, I'll grab a sandwich back at the room.'

This is the seething Medusa of human comfort zones, a jellyfish combat of fallacies, biases, black-and-white thinking and moral high ground, with which the table has not only maintained a routine but a delicate status quo. All are thus satisfied. The Medusa has lied, leveraged, appealed for allies against each of its writhing coils. And like rams testing their rank, having established the correct order of things, all present can retire to fine-tune their status, pairing off to project their behaviours as flaws onto their friends.

Such is bourgeois life, if not human life.

Everything seems to have an immune system. Groups, institutions and cultures have one that works just like the body's own, in their case invisibly targeting ideas and shifts in the status quo. The mind's drive to reduce chaos calls other brains to join it in subjective consensus over what it feels are threats, whether they logically are or not. Academia does it, science does it, we do it.

This is the crap we deal with every day.

If we huddle inside a group repelling ideas from outside, then the group's strongest members will most often hold sway. If we step outside, we feel the special sting of their Medusa, as arguments against our apartness lose their reason until finally any nearby stone will do as a weapon. This is justified by the immune system, which draws a line above the arguments that put us outside it, relegating our ideas to a category worthy of attack by any means. It's a quarantine like the conspiracy theorist box, an anti-category that is a modern equivalent of heresy: just as telling fortunes was once indicative of also casting spells, denying the dangers of sugar can now also make you a climate-change sceptic. In terms of immune systems quarantining ideas within categories above argument – which can contain as much unrelated shit as your kitchen drawer – the equivalent in the physical world today is the Terrorism Act, which like its international counterparts replaces the Witchcraft Act as the category where a suspect's rights can be waived in the absence of a crime; ideas and circumstance will do.

Recognising this phenomenon can be a goldmine for writing narratives. A character's ideas, even simple ones such as how to approach the bank for a loan, can be ruthlessly cut down by an immune system before he even leaves the house, as one white cell reacts at the kitchen table, calls in others to press home the attack, then distorts the argument to destroy everything around the idea, including its designer's good character. The gold lies in the fallacies they use, the strength of their attack, previous errors they can wield as ammunition, because through these we expose the deeper motivations of the Medusas in our book, without simply recounting what they're like. The notion of interactive immune systems can build roads deep into character, filling human drama with life; plus it makes the eavesdropping genuine.

It was uncommon before the mid-nineteenth century to expose a character's thoughts and biases in fiction, novels kept to more physical interactions. The likes of Fyodor Dostoevsky changed the landscape, writing psychology into his stories before the science was even around. Watch him set up bad blood between these characters as they manoeuvre, trying to exclude the narrator – the most unpleasant of them all – from a dinner date in the 1864 novella *Notes from Underground*:

One of Simonov's two guests was Ferfichkin, a Russified German of short height with the face of a monkey, a mocking fool, my nastiest enemy since early schooldays, a vulgar, impertinent braggart who played at being most delicately conceited but was of course a little coward to his depths. He was among the worshippers of Zverkov, who played up to him with ulterior motives and often borrowed money from him. Simonov's other guest, Trudolyubov, was an unremarkable personage, a military fellow, tall, with a cold physiognomy, rather honest, but one who bowed down before success of all kinds and was only capable of discussing promotions. He was some kind of distant relative of Zverkov's and this, it is silly to say, accorded him a certain significance among us. He always thought little of me; he behaved towards me not exactly politely but tolerably.

'So, now, with seven roubles each,' said Trudolyubov, 'between the three of us that's twenty-one roubles – and for that you can dine well. Zverkov, of course, won't pay.'

'Yes, of course, we'll be inviting him,' Simonov resolved.

'You can't really think,' Ferfichkin meddled haughtily and fervently, just like an obnoxious lackey who boasts about his master the general's medals, 'you don't really think that Zverkov will let us pay for him? He will accept out of delicacy but he'll lay on a half-dozen bottles himself.'

'What will we do with a half-dozen between four?' Trudolyubov remarked, paying attention only to the question of the half-dozen bottles.

'So that's three of us, with Zverkov makes four, twenty-one roubles at the Hôtel de Paris, tomorrow at five o'clock,' Simonov concluded, finally, having been picked as the master of ceremonies.

'How's that twenty-one roubles?' I asked with a certain agitation, acting as though I was offended. 'If you count me too then it wouldn't be twenty-one but twenty-eight roubles.'

It seemed to me that my sudden and unexpected proposal would seem quite gracious and they would all be convinced at once, and would look upon me with respect.

'So you want to join?' Simonov remarked with displeasure, somehow avoiding looking at me. He knew me by heart.

And it drove me wild that he knew me by heart.

'And why not, sir? It seems I'm also a friend, and I confess that I was offended to be excluded,' I said, starting to seethe again.

'And where should we have found you?' Ferfichkin jumped in, rudely.

'You were always at odds with Zverkov,' added Trudolyubov, frowning.

But I had already latched on and wouldn't let it go.

'It seems to me that no one has the right to judge,' I retorted with a tremble in my voice, as though God-knows-what had happened. 'It may be exactly because we were at odds that I want to join you now.'

'Well, who can make you out . . . with such lofty ideas?' Trudolyubov smirked.

Writers are also personally subject to immune systems if or when they finally mention their work to someone else. Imagine trying to hawk a synopsis where a twister blows a farmhouse from Kansas to a land of singing midgets. Or one where the protagonist stays at home and describes all the books on his shelves. Or for that matter a comedy about a high-school massacre. Nobody would've accepted them – they had to be explained as books, had to gel by themselves, create their own climates and worlds; at which they were admitted by an immune system and absorbed into the culture.

Unlike the tableful of holidaymakers:

'Old Ken chucked his toys out of the pram tonight.'

'I know, I've never had a bad chop at the sausage place.'

'You know what it's really about – that lecture he got from the waiter.'

'I know, insecurity.'

'Wonder how they're getting on with Polynesian.'

'Rice coming out of their bloody ears.'

'Sandwich?'

'Where's the room-service menu . . .?'

The conscious and intelligent manipulation of the organised habits and opinions of the masses is an important element in democratic society.

Edward Bernays

18 REALITY

Whatever that is. Take Darren, one of a tight band of friends in Cornwall, where the laws of physics work differently. Darren can always be relied upon for an intelligent drink, he undertakes the job like a man building a chemistry set for a child. As a result he collects anecdotes like nobody else, witnessed by many, enough to fill every evening you see him without ever being repeated. Look at just one of them, the most recent I heard: it isn't unusual during a big night out for Darren to forget where he left his car or motorbike. Once this was known to the rest of the gang they also made sport of moving and hiding his cars and motorbikes. So that when he woke one day to find his bike missing he first called the usual suspects, who claimed to know nothing, then waited three more days before reporting it to the police.

This time the bike had genuinely been stolen. After reporting it he gradually forgot it and moved house. Then, months later, driving through town without a seatbelt, a patrol car followed him into a lane and pulled him over to book him. After checking his licence the officer said, 'Been looking for you – we recovered your bike.'

The punchline: whoever stole the bike had invested in it, and the thing came back in better condition than it had gone in. The laws of Cornish physics.

I bring it up because unless we write Cornish comedies

it would be hard to justify true stories like this in fiction. It's one of the ironies of the modern day that the truly real is often too implausible to include in fiction. There's no longer a 'real' in the sense there used to be, the laces of reason have come undone and made naturalism of satire. So we have to judge reality carefully, make minimal use of coincidence in writing, because ironically we won't tolerate in fiction what we tolerate and even enjoy in life. This is doubly true if we want to flirt around the edges of the absurd, as I discovered when I started to research the themes behind *Vernon God Little*. If anything, a satire has to sail closer to truth than other fiction to really bite, so I needed to find some truths behind gun crime, the death penalty and the lobby for televised executions, among other things. But the facts that I found were often too ridiculous to use.

The background was sadly predictable: in the USA you can be put to death for more than fifty types of crime. Texas executes more offenders than the other thirty-eight death-penalty states put together, and a defendant is between four and eleven times more likely to be executed for murdering a white person than a black person. In the year I began to write, there were 11,000 attacks with weapons in US schools, and in the preceding ten years the number of children under the age of thirteen arrested for firearms possession had risen from 10,000 to 100,000 nationally. Execution of juveniles was then on the decrease in most countries, and more than seventy active death-penalty countries had abolished it for offenders under eighteen. Nevertheless, in the fifteen years leading up to writing *Vernon*, nine countries still carried out juvenile executions:

Bangladesh (1)	Barbados (1)
Iran (unknown)	Iraq (at least 13)
Nigeria (1)	Pakistan (4)
Saudi Arabia (1)	Yemen (1)
USA (9)	

Not only had the USA continued to execute juveniles but they were the fastest growing population on death row. Even an intellectually disabled youngster had been executed, despite it being known that his disabilities could lead to him signing false confessions. The facts were eye-opening, hard work to absorb. My novel's absurd premise grew more realistic and plausible *provided I didn't use the real facts, which were unbelievable.* It turned out I could tick every thematic box: there was a well-backed lobby for the televising of executions, the justice system in Texas had recently launched a fast-track programme for death-sentence trials, partly reflecting the fact that it costs 'ten times more', according to a former American jurist, to execute someone than to imprison them for life, owing to longer and costlier appeals – some taking up to twenty years – and higher security and service costs for death-row inmates compared to regular prisoners. Added to scenarios like that, the percentage of patently unsafe convictions made it easy to imagine an onlooker railroaded to death for someone else's crime – moreover it had already happened. It was a perfect storm in terms of *Vernon*'s plot, but some people still call the book outrageous. Look at some of the shit I couldn't use:

The same month that the book was published, complaints by the father of a boy being prosecuted in a death-penalty trial in Louisiana were upheld against local prosecutors who were appearing in court wearing joke neckties: one a bright red tie featuring a hangman's noose, another sporting the Grim Reaper. In the prosecutors' defence it was noted that they had stopped throwing death-sentence parties upon conviction, although a tradition of gifting plaques with lethal injections engraved above the convict's name might still go on today. Some jurisdictions in Texas threw steak and Jim Beam parties after a conviction. One district attorney hung a noose above her office door for decoration, another founded the Silver Needle Society. The assistant attorney-general of one southern state kept a toy electric chair on his desk that buzzed and lit up. Not to mention one man's request to smoke a cigarette before execution – turned down on the grounds that it was bad for his health.

Among specific trials I looked at, black suspects were executed for crimes witnesses had attributed to white people; suspects were picked out of police line-ups in which they alone were wearing handcuffs, one was even put to death despite the crime's victims swearing he wasn't the perpetrator.

As well as being grotesque it's all strangely useless when trying to give a believable taste to a culture in a book. We don't care as much about the unbelievable, it's just too damn unbelievable. It falls to us not only to separate real and unreal in existential life, to inspect it and see what's really happening, but to control the real in fiction and often tone it down. Books have a greater duty to inspire trust through plausibility, or at least to set up worlds where the outrageous can seem plausible in its context. If we build a world where pangolins rule Manhattan, it's not implausible for a piano to fall on one. But then if a piano fell on a pangolin on 10th Street, it wouldn't be implausible for him to remain unharmed and walk away either; and if he can do that he can also play Debussy. See the problem? If I write a court scene where the district attorney wears a noose necktie, we don't care as much about our defendant because the narrative odds are ridiculously stacked against him. If there are noose neckties in the book, he could just as easily escape on a donkey. Reality can be nonsense. Don't get me wrong, I wanted to flirt with the absurd, and did – but not *that* fucking absurd. When we want to transmit a gut response, a feeling at the end of a book like reaching the beach after a pounding at sea – our chosen beach, our chosen sea – we often have to build it from different and lesser things than absolute truth. Then curiously, in our choice of details, in the measure of our judgement and the alchemy of the writing, a whole truth might sparkle through. The question of reality also throws up a decision as soon as we're piqued by some outrageous theme: if the detail is really that scandalous, come back over the border and write it as non-fiction. Although it's a measure of how resilient the governing fictions of our time can be that even when we write a new truth, it doesn't change popular history. Look up the Falklands war and read how deliberately Argentina invaded those islands. Then note the more recently written truth that says the Argentine invasion party first spotted on the islands – the sighting that kicked off the war – was in fact a Buenos Aires salvage merchant's team under contract to the British Embassy to dismantle an abandoned whaling station. History erased that part of the story. When Britain phoned Buenos Aires and said get your men off our island, the Argentine government rightly asked, 'What men?' We must've called them liars, they must've called us liars, neither side stood down, and the rest is history. I don't doubt that tensions were in the air at the time. But the story of the salvage merchant and his job were forgotten in the fracas. In real life, having invested to secure the British contract, he quietly went broke and remained unknown until a *New Yorker* journalist picked up the trail and wrote the story.

And that was purely innocent history; where outright deceit is concerned, the first Gulf war was only narrowly authorised by US Congress after a sobbing fifteen-year-old Kuwaiti girl testified that hundreds of babies were being torn from hospital incubators and killed by Iraqi forces. That news galvanised the world. The US president repeatedly quoted the girl while building support for war, citing exact numbers – 312 babies tossed from incubators and left to die. Respected human rights groups spread the outrage, and the war duly went ahead on the strength of it.

But a later written truth says Kuwait didn't have more than a handful of incubators, and no babies were torn from them. The girl was a daughter of Kuwait's ambassador to the US.

A region was demolished over it. This is the world we have to fictionalise plausibly, a place where, for all intents and purposes, no closely examined story lives up to its accepted history. There's plenty of elbow room for us in there. It was the satirist Tom Lehrer who, after Henry Kissinger bagged the Nobel Peace Prize, said, 'It was at that moment that satire died.'

Can we show otherwise?

Bring on the laws of Cornish physics.

There is only one plot – things are not what they seem.

Jim Thompson

19 SYMBOLS

I stayed in a patch of English countryside full of trees and
birds. After a while the songs and calls became familiar
and my mind filtered them out. Then one morning a new
bird sang, or maybe a regular bird sang a new song. I tried
to see which bird it was, because the song was unusual. It
started with a single note cleanly rising and falling, then
a burst of quick modulations. The bird stayed around
singing that call every day. There was something weird
about it, I couldn't think what.

Then one day, for some reason, I paid new attention to
a common background sound, filtered until then. It was a
police car speeding down a motorway in the middle distance; and that was the song the bird had picked up, the
routine rise and fall of a siren.

I never saw which bird it was.

I called it the emergency bird.

✑✑✑

In the mysterious way that we sometimes show glimpses
of unconscious sensitivity, to the invisible language of
chemistry and who knows what else, glimpses like the
occasional breaker that sucks out a flash of the seabed
before crashing, the first three girls I ever went out with
were drawn to a gift their predecessor had given me,

in the form of a shirt. The first girl gave me a tropical shirt, which hung with a few I owned; and the second one, without a word and without knowing where it had come from, commandeered that shirt for herself. Before she moved on she bought me her choice of shirt – and the next girl immediately became attached to it, without reference to any of my other things, and without saying why. It could be that they shared a taste, but it felt as if they could sense the hand of a previous girl, obliterating it by taking over the territory of the shirt. I have none of the shirts bought for me back then; all went with the girl following the one who had bought them.

Over four weeks of autumn between my first novel being shortlisted and finally winning the Man Booker Prize, a curious thing happened in a downstairs bathroom of my house. Butterflies would appear and fly around my head when I went in for a crap. They would come out one by one. Strange, because their season was gone, there were none outside in nature, only in that toilet. But they wouldn't appear if I went in to take a leak. Now: the door was shut, they didn't come from outside. I couldn't see where they came from, and when I left the room they would stay there, flying. But the next time I came in they would be gone; unless I came in for a crap, in which case they appeared again and flew around my head. It was a mystery. If I stayed there long enough, five would come out. It became predictable enough that I took a new pleasure in going to sit and think with the butterflies. If you believed in omens they seemed good ones.

After the prize I returned home to find they had gone. One day, much later, I solved the mystery: an old tooth-brush mug had been exiled to the top of the bathroom cabinet. They had lived in the mug, maybe attracted by toothpaste. When the light had been on long enough – not so quick as when I took a leak – they must have thought it was their day in the sun and come out to fly around.

Poor bastards.

I had a dream when I was five, of the type that never goes away, a hyper-real experience with more feeling and tex-ture than life. In the dream, I had just climbed into a car after a family picnic. My mother was driving. As I settled into the back I realised my father wasn't there. Through the rear window I could see a wooded glen where we had been, and beside it a rock face with a cave entrance. I saw broad stone stairs spiralling up into the dark, and for an instant saw my father's heel vanishing up them. Then my mother started the car and began to pull away. I reminded her that we had left my father behind but she ignored me and drove on. The dream's overwhelming legacy was a feeling of helpless loss. As the clearing and the cave fell away I thought I saw a rag doll flung limply down the stairs where he had been. But I couldn't be sure. What I can be sure of is that those images set processes moving which had to do with fear and darkness and which never went away. It doesn't matter what they meant, the feelings had their own intelligence and were clear. It wasn't enough to write them off as a dream, they were too concrete; whether or not they had meaning, they came full of a sense that they were not only meaningful but crucial.

From the Bogey Man to the Grim Reaper, life is more comfortable when we don't address darkness point-blank. Perhaps that subconscious theatre is active from birth, maybe it even springs from that speechlessness, that powerlessness to act. I say subconscious because it seems that symbols are native to dreams, I don't feel they're a learned response. Perhaps they live in all kinds of creatures focusing perceptions of threat, as if we're born with dormant hens inside to react to the dark on our behalf. We feel them scatter without knowing what set them off. We just know it's dark, and shudder.

Perhaps then as artists some of us spend a life painting hens instead of dark. A hooded man with a scythe becomes poetry.

I was reminded at Tobias's cemetery exhibition that the Grim Reaper is a relatively new symbol. Before him the most common symbol for death was a woman. In Europe she would arrive for a dance, and we would 'dance with death'. I also saw an old painting showing soap bubbles rising into the dark behind a skull. A perfect symbol: some bubbles would grow big, some would fly high, some would float to the ground – but all would pop and not a thing in their natures could tell us when.

This all came to mind because art and literature deal

with what's beneath, they run on symbols. And I came to wonder if that first memorable dream wasn't a first literary experience. If maybe the same processes involved in the dream were behind the nature of writing. As it is, no matter how self-consciously I write, I always find symbols and ironies creeping into the work by themselves, often beyond my understanding. And yet they make their own sense, and paint feelings in keeping with the life of the narrative. They're organic, beyond calculation and craft, but are somehow central to the experience being written. As applied symbols go, many acknowledge that *Godzilla* was symbolic of Japan's wartime terror; less remember that in its original form the monster *Gojira* was nuclear-powered, taking its strength from atomic tests in the Pacific and unleashing this power upon Japan. Conceived in the period between the atomic bombing of Hiroshima and Nagasaki, and the deployment of the more lethal hydrogen bomb, the film was the first of many monster films through which the Japanese came into touch with and purged their fears of nuclear annihilation.

Enough art deals with death and sex that those twin demons may underpin all subconscious life. As to whether symbols have applied meaning, as to whether they assuage, purge or prepare us for anything, it's arguable. Maybe the key lies in our sensitivity to them. But the more you notice them, the stronger they get. Many years after this inner life began, I was again in a car driven by my mother. My father was terminally ill. The family had reached that stage in his care where it saw fit to take a break and do something else. I didn't buy it. We didn't see him that day. We left him alone living hours we could never replace. It felt wrong. Then, as we pulled away from traffic lights, I saw rising in a dark face beside us was the hospital where he lay I looked back knowing that I'd done it before.

Maybe symbols are the gloves we use to pat the unapproachable. Maybe books are where we store the gloves. Symbols love being written. Design one, and a bunch of others creep in out of nowhere. Maybe they're a nest egg.

However it works, I only ever feel responsible for half the symbols in a book.

The rest come out like butterflies if I sit long enough.

I may not have gone where I intended to go, but I think I have ended up where I needed to be.

Douglas Adams

20 WEAKNESS

Look at your life. See honestly how much of it derives from compulsion, wrong thinking and weakness, and how much from purpose and strength. Put aside the compensating systems that balance things up so we can even drag ourselves out of bed in the morning – and look. Unwanted pregnancy, failed relationship, debt crisis, family feud, grinding job, dangerous romance; all things we can rationalise as part of life's rich tapestry and edit to seem like purposeful strides. But one day look at it really. The unwanted pregnancy is because we were too compulsive getting laid. The relationship failed because we fell too much for that one little thing and used all our imagination making the rest of him or her look great. The debt crisis, well, we felt the big break was just around the corner and, anyway, we deserved those bargains. The family feud because we refuse to adjust the position we decided on when we were six, which was that everyone else could get fucked. The grinding job because it's just so much fucking easier to do it and complain than to take a plunge into the abyss of what we really want, and maybe fail there too. The dangerous romance is just our demons running amok to show us what puppets we are and who really pulls the strings.

I'll say it for myself: to the extent that I have had any influence over the course of my life, it has mostly been influenced by weakness. Which is ironic, because I've always had purposeful dreams. As to whether any good came of it so far, sure, some did – but the best good came from writing about weakness.

So the thing is this: the direction of affluent life in the modern day is vastly more driven by weakness than by strength. Over the course of a century the markets have learned to prey in clinical detail on weakness and insecurity and, moreover, have learned how to create them where they didn't necessarily exist. Once upon a time, we had to develop individual justifying mechanisms to cover our shit and make our issues look like some kind of positive action and informed free choice, and we did it, we're good at that. Now we don't even have to do that; the markets and the medical-pharmaceutical complex do it for us, we can buy self-esteem and forgiveness.

In a climate where weakness is life, the only thing we need to do to be extraordinary is to admit it. This is what we can do in writing. It makes writing relevant because underneath all the gloss we're still fragile and curious and waiting. A book can reach through, it's not a public event but a personal one. For us it's about remembering to speak to the soul inside. If you were thinking of square-jawed heroes in your book, in they go, for sure – but they should also be weak. Their heroism need only consist of overcoming weakness once, for a minute – the right minute, the last minute. Then they'll be real. Then they're one of us. Then it's the story we've been telling and retelling since before we moved out of caves: not of a perennial hero but of one who conquers a flaw when it counts.

It's perfect because we all warm to someone like ourselves, even more so to someone struggling more than us with the same weaknesses. In writing it can be as simple as showing a character's susceptibility to everyday snags, few things attract empathy as quickly as someone in a bad spot. It's not enough to have the Terminator stride into a supermarket, we need to see his card declined at the checkout.

Against this, there really are people who purposefully build their whole dreams. They're not our dreams, we could easier build someone else's than our own, but some people do build their own. Some people also will never have a card declined, a bad romance, a dull job. But these are people in a safe tidal pool away from life's stream, whether they admirably construct and maintain it, or whether it's a pool of rare luck. They're pointless in writing unless we obstruct or destroy them. And there's something in how much fun it is to obstruct them that also reeks of humanity. There's something in our lust for conflict that reeks of it, and there's strength in our admitting that we want equally to nurture and destroy things.

This is the bare, electric, indifferent heart of life.

What writing must really be for.

When we look beneath the obvious as writers a new palette of colours shows up to paint with, because nobody goes around showing their weakness. In the tics we've developed across a lifetime to rationalise and hide our flaws are all the real voices of a story.

My old man said that the last thing he remembered was everyone looking strangely at him across the boardroom table. It was at a UN meeting in New York, nothing new to him. He collapsed at the table. He was younger than I am today and woke up in the New York Hospital, where they went over him with a fine-tooth comb; but he looked fine to them and soon came home.

My old man had suffered headaches for all the time I knew him, which was sixteen years by then. Not frequent, in fact rare; but strong. The worst I can remember was once when he took me fishing to an island and spent the whole time on his bed in the dark. After the New York thing he got one again, then another, and within a few months was back in the hospital for tests. Brain tumour. That's all I heard. But the surgeon was great, flew his own plane down from the slopes, talked science with my dad, the whole affair was one of hundred-dollar pills, Burt Bacharach in the coffee shop of the hotel I went to live in for a while on 51st Street, and hope. After all, this great surgeon was flying down from the slopes.

Fast-forward three years and many seasons later, of experimental drugs, miraculous cures, brutal relapses, Burt Bacharach giving way to the Sex Pistols – and the old man was suddenly well enough to feel that he should visit old friends. He went on tour, went back to his Alma Mater, visited his family. Soon after that it took a doctor in another hospital far away to tell us that he wouldn't survive the week. My family didn't believe the doctor. Burt Bacharach was still around, Manhattan still existed, surgeons still flew down from the slopes, wiry Irish girls and stained Cubans serving melted cheese and ketchup in the coffee shops of 51st Street still said everything would be fine. But the doctor said forget it. The old man wouldn't make it to New York. He would miss any future burnished American wood panelling, automatic ice-water, easy listening and the ride of Turbo-Hydramatic gearboxes in limousines. In not so many words the doctor said this. He gave us to understand it because he was a busy and practical person who didn't deal in illusions. He didn't fly himself down from any slopes. He never saw happy hour on West 51st and 7th. My mother was fucking offended, as if shattering the illusion would be what killed the old man. But I got it. On his last day I sat by his bed and told him all the things that ended up being lies, about all the kids I'd name after him and how much honour I would try to do him, and he squeezed my hand as if understanding. For all I know those were the last words he ever heard.

Then, just as in all good hospitals, he was quietly killed by nurses administering a routine procedure which they knew he wouldn't survive.

He never told anyone he would die. He didn't tell himself. He bequeathed nothing, left no will, cancelled no subscriptions, paid no bills, left no instructions or notes. But we found a letter in his files from the first New York doctor, three years before; a terse, factual letter telling him that his was a tumour which nobody had survived for more than three years. Now: this was a man who strongly believed in the power of the mind, and who used his mind to brilliant effect in his life. Moreover, these were the heydays of positive thinking, before cynicism was fashionable, back when defiance made you a hippy and stubble made you an immigrant.

For our purposes, thinking about characters in writing, the question is: did he show weakness or strength? Did he bravely shoot the finger at Fate, or did he just stick his head in the sand? These are the choices in the story, no matter how broadly we consider the question it will weigh into one or the other answer via the information I choose to include. Although novels aren't about answers but questions, and our information has to be the ride in itself, we'll still know which way our character is leaning.

How would you tell it? Strength or weakness?

Here's the information the story needs, also from real life; not an answer but an angle that makes the question sparkle. As a young man my father was an air force pilot. He joined on his eighteenth birthday, and his above-average night-vision routed him to night bombers. World War Two was on and those planes were going down like raindrops. His chances of surviving a tour of duty were one in three, which in the practical world of military administration threw up some issues. One of these was the amount of lockers that had to be broken open and ruined when a lost airman's belongings were returned to next of kin. So the golden rule before every mission was to leave your locker key behind.

My old man never did.

The moral for writing: don't explain a character.

Show us what moulds him.

PART THREE

TOOLBOX

From the moment I picked up your book until I laid it down, I was convulsed with laughter. Some day I intend reading it.

Groucho Marx

21 DEFINITIONS

This is what I understand to be good writing by current standards. We don't have to follow any of it, but if we swim against the school we still need to know where it's pointed. It's what your how-to-write books will tell you, which means a convention of editors more than writers. A lot of it is how to suck eggs, but even the obvious stuff is worth going over again, it pulls it to mind where we need it. We're here uploading, after all. None of these parameters are intimidating, and they all work. If your ideas can conform to these guidelines you'll be a good writer by current standards, which are a set of ideas that hasn't changed in a hundred years. Some, like economy in writing, are obvious. Others are more about the reader's experience, and are worthwhile if you want to be read. Books, like movies, have a structural language that readers are used to, and upsetting that language imposes a workload, which in an editor's mind will impose a cost. Most arguments at the theoretical end of literature are to do with whether that language best reflects life. My position is that it no longer does, but the form of the novel is still powerful, and fun. Until you come up with a new form, it's what we have. Working down from the top, this is roughly where we're at:

Novels today still tend to be modernist, which among other things means they have defined beginnings and middles, and seek to neatly resolve a story at the end. They not only tell of external events but explore a character's subjective thoughts. Modernism in literature grew as a reaction to nineteenth-century realism, which was more about the external story. Postmodernism grew as a reaction to modernism, and throws out the rules of any defined form or structure. If you're a postmodernist you don't need any information so I'll skip it here. The periods of these forms roughly correspond to the last two centuries, but within their definitions there are modern works from as far back as ancient Rome, and postmodern books from centuries ago. If you want to write fiction then where we are today is still modern.

And in that case the animal thinks like this:

FICTION

Anything made up. It can be about you in real-life situations and still be fiction if you tart it up. It can be about things that happened to Abraham Lincoln and be fiction. But I refer to the opening chapter and say that fact and fiction are increasingly blurred, news and entertainment are converging. Thus writing something real poses new challenges, as the real grows more fictional anyway. Also irony grows trickier as our tolerance of the absurd in real life increases.

NON-FICTION

Anything not made up. Essays, journalism, factual books, textbooks are all professional non-fiction writing and have to be true to the letter. They can still benefit from fiction techniques to keep them interesting, but if we weren't in the Gulf war we can't write an otherwise factual piece that says we were. If in doubt over how much you can fudge a viewpoint or guess any facts, call it fiction, or faction. One way to get busted in writing is by dressing ideas as facts.

COMMERCIAL

Writing crafted to give readers a good ride and a satisfying payoff, which means crafted to sell. It's driven by story and is a job of plotting for effect. Commercial fiction includes the popular genres of crime, romance, thriller, fantasy and sci-fi. There's a sweet overlap between commercial and literary fiction, with some great literary novels that are excitingly plotted, and commercial books that trawl deeper themes. I make a distinction between commercial and literary but it's not to minimise commercial writing; if anything it's the more learned form, and the harder to perfect from the outset. With commercial novels you're competing against master craftspeople. In the context of this book I refer to literary fiction as tricky because it more often draws from dark places, and its very lack of practical definition can drive you mad. But that's a different kind of tricky to writing well – and we all face that challenge together.

LITERARY

Literary writing is driven more by characters and ideas. It doesn't have to be exciting or conform to formulas, it can reflect and enrich by opening a window on some human theme. And it can be self-indulgent, it can be about your navel. The simplest definition: commercial is about story, literary about character; although both are more satisfying if a character is changed by the effects of a story. For me the best book is one that draws from both forms, a structure that pumps us through big human ideas.

ECONOMY

The best writing in all forms, except premium supermarket ready-meal advertising and exposed-brick gastro-victim bistro-menu design, is accepted to be economical (unlike this sentence). Most of the greatest modern writers are those who managed to say the biggest things with the fewest words. The notion of economy includes the choice of plain over complicated words: 'hard' is stronger than 'difficult', 'dead' more resonant than 'deceased'. The old chestnut is: 'Don't use a ten-dollar word when a five-cent word will do.' Weeding out redundant or clunky words can be fun, when you have a big enough mass to survive the loss. Most sentences in first draft can lose at least a third of their words, and over time we grow an eye for the ones that need to go: any that repeat another word or idea, any unnecessary adjectives or adverbs – plus teachers have spent the last hundred years saying never write 'very' or 'quite' unless it's a character's voice in dialogue.

Much of the headfuck of trying to write well is in this

whittling, and in keeping the page rhythmic with sentences of different lengths, making a heartbeat from short and long lines, commas and semi-colons. I haven't written especially economically, but I admit the results are impressive when you try it. Many of my sentences in first draft can lose half their words without getting down to the bone. That distillation reveals the book.

To play Hemingway, take a sentence like this: 'Raúl realised that he might have killed the man, he didn't seem to be moving very much any more.'

Then imagine him with it: 'Raúl killed him. The man was still.' More than anything else, economy can make your writing look as if somebody else wrote it – as in a writer. We don't think about it in a first draft, we write shit with the confidence that it'll change. Just rip every third word out of a sentence and see. Also embraced by this idea is the notion of killing your babies: anything we've written that doesn't move the story forward is redundant, no matter how enchanting.

EXPOSITION

Show, don't tell. This may be the biggest problem with fiction manuscripts. The best quote is Chekhov's: *'Don't tell me the moon is shining; show me the glint of light on broken glass.'* It seems obvious but in reality it's easier to tell than to show, it's what we do in speech. Creative writing is the art of suggestion, which is what makes it powerful; we're not creating images but suggestions that provoke them. It's what makes a book unique and personal to everyone who reads it. We don't passively absorb a narrative as we do watching a movie, we build it in our minds as if we were there. Once you pocket that idea it's easier to imagine the kind of sketching we have to do, which also means not too much. There are important books that spend half a chapter describing a door, but the recommended path for us is to open the thing and step through. Which leads to the next imperative in the holy trinity:

FLOW

Don't stop. Throw the narrative in motion from the first sentence, preferably with a bang, then make everything that follows move it forward. Describe the door when a character knocks, the porch light as a shadow moves behind it. Don't stop to describe a character, show her through actions: 'Even barefoot she walked on high heels.' Make every word count. Allied to this is the rule that says use active rather than passive sentences – not 'drinks were brought' but 'he brought drinks'. Obviously a story isn't all action, later on we'll see where to put the adagios; but even then we can't hang around smelling too many roses.

Enough rules. Inside them lives the gamut of modern techniques, for plotting, tension, characterisation and the rest. We'll deal with them one by one.

For now just grow inklings of how it can all fit your story.

A movie grants a visa. A book makes you a citizen.

DBC Pierre

22   BURNING DESIRE

Hearing that stronger is better in fiction can make you feel that every book has to be a thriller in order to work, that our story about the cabbage-worm will need a gun in it to get anywhere, but that's not the case. It's a question of subjectivity: the child's desire to own a puppy is as strong as some maniac's desire to destroy the city. We can make a snail's passage across a floor more significant in the way we present it, and that's what the following tools are about. The first and most important idea, worthy of a page on its own, is to define for our characters – snails, cabbage-worms or heroes – strong enough desires that we feel all the obstacles they face. Their desire should be expressed as early as possible in a story, and should optimally be restated at the top of every chapter in the form of a desire for that chapter. This is a story's pump. It sets a goal which becomes our goal, but it can't just be any old wish: it should be a burning desire. The snail has to *really* want to cross the floor, or, better still, has to *need* to. Characters' desires can be ambitions, escapes or compulsions, any condition compelling enough to make plausible their will to overcome at all costs. Then every obstacle we throw at them, every reversal, every enemy is something we'll feel in the gut.

Desire is the heart of all action, the engine that drives a story.

O villain, villain, smiling, damned villain!

William Shakespeare

23 OPPOSING FORCE

The opposite force, responsible for the other half of a story's internal combustion. An antagonist's power can fluctuate above or below a hero's as a narrative unfolds, but it'll generally be in charge until the climax. As a force against desire it should seem insurmountable, which means that our snail hits the breakfast bar before he's even halfway across the room; not only an impenetrable vertical surface but a mile of inset shelving with an over-hang at the top. And it shouldn't even just be that simple: the love of his life is leaving on a bus from the other side in under two hours – *for ever*.

Antagonists embody power. Matching or exceeding the strength of a protagonist's desire means they can't just be bad, they can't be simple obstructions or irritants. Antagonists really fuck things up. They should stop at nothing. They can take the form of specific enemies or impossible conditions, or they can be embodiments of a character's own miscalculations; he thought the breakfast bar was only six inches high. It means antagonists can also come as internal weaknesses and demons, our novel about the addict doesn't need outside enemies, the addict is the enemy.

In classical tales of yore, where these ideas came from, the protagonist and antagonist often start a story as friends, even brothers, where we see their innocent natures and powers at play. Then something happens to make them rivals – their love for the same person, joining opposite armies at war, a family feud – and they must face each other in conflict, all the more bitter for their knowledge of each other and the force of their underlying love. From the outset we know who the hero is – he's the one with the noble cause, while the other one turns into a dick. Their powers may rise and fall at first but the antagonist soon has the upper hand and grows it to overwhelming force. By the final scene the hero's desires are beaten and hopeless; but in whatever made him the weaker – something we've seen demonstrated earlier – he finds the keys to new strength, rising up at the last minute to win the day.

It can seem contrived, but a story's heart lies in its characters. We want to know them inside out, which means testing the pants off them, watching them perform. We get to do it best when we pit mad desires against bastard foes.

It's no easy business to be simple.

Gustave Flaubert

24 SEASONS

I want to separate the job of writing into two parts. Two seasons, because they each call on different feelings and psychologies, and each suits a different frame of mind. In the northern hemisphere I find they actually fit to winter and summer, the first better for long winter nights, the next good for long daylight.

The first season is the one we just looked at, of speed and abandon. Of art. The second is of carpentry and structure. In some respects to write the way I'll propose is to do it backwards – that is, to jump in before we know what we're doing, then go back and make it look like we did. Sure, we'll roughly know when we first sit down what kind of animal we're out to write – but there are benefits, and I think a better chance of extraordinary work, if we leave the job open to make its own way to places we can't yet see, let characters drive it there chasing their passions.

You'll gather that the season of speed is for the first draft. It presupposes that we tend to overthink things, tend to become rigid or fall prey to demons who don't want our work to go ahead. And it presupposes that inside us are things which will bring our writing to life, things we can't calculate and are unaware of. In many cases, and I think especially today, we have to trick ourselves into being free. There's so much complexity behind our conformities that escaping can take strategy and craftiness.

We're justified in using whatever tools we can find to let our mind empty itself onto a page and show us in turn what it consists of. So this first half of the job is exponential – the more abandon we can apply to a first draft, the more we learn where the book wants to go. So we follow it and learn even more.

After that we come to the summer of the work.

The time to begin writing an article is when you have finished it to your satisfaction. By that time you begin to clearly and logically perceive what it is you really want to say.

Mark Twain

25 CARPENTRY

There's barely a thing under the sun that can't be made an analogy of for the experience of a book. It's a journey, a garden, a mansion, a swim, a mirror, a road. But here's the wash: the writer has to consciously build it that way. It can be all those things, but not by accident. This was the part of the job that set me back at first. It was fine to just rave and flow through a voice, I'm glad I did it before any of this more fastidious shit slowed me down. But then I had to make it work.

Building a good read around your art uses different routines. Opposite skills in some ways. It's where the conscious comes in, where we get down to the more disciplined grind of writing. But it's fun; with a pile of clay before you whose nuggets are the spirit of a book, it can be the biggest buzz of the job. You give it shape, cut out the cringes, siphon excess. If you're me, characters' names change five times apiece, I try cutting chapters in different places. I get the weight and feel of what I have and what it needs to be. And what I have is a pile of timber – or clay, or plants, or asphalt, or whatever analogy you have in mind. This phase is the first time you'll feel traction, see real effects on the work. In time it won't look like you wrote it.

I was someone who would rather have written a first draft with my eyes shut and never shown it to anyone. I could say I'd written a book, and there it was. I sense that a lot of us would rather do this with our eyes shut, just hammer something out and grow a romance with it as it is. Otherwise we have to admit that our first attempt can be mostly crap. It's uncomfortable. But after hooking onto some writing in my first draft that I actually liked, I knew I couldn't take the chicken-shit way out. The risk-averse way. Instead I could turn it into a real book and take my chances that it would still be crap. It would be up to me. And actually when the thing came out there were plenty who still thought it was crap – but not all. And that's the best we can ever hope for.

Structure is an admission that we want someone to read the work – to understand it as we did, and relish it. Raging helter-skelter through a first draft was for us; structure is for them, and the more confidently we lay it out the more they'll trust the invitation into our madness. It took a while to get my head around the techniques behind this. I had to bow to the physical craft of it and admit I was starting from scratch. All the monkeys on my back had to climb aboard this agenda. And they did, and what soon turned me into a lover of this phase was the speed with which things improved. Literally before my eyes: tension increased by ending chapters here rather than there, sentences grew strong by losing words, pages tightened as dull paragraphs fell out. I focused on meaning and forward motion, everything had to push the narrative or it was out. If I paused for poetry, reflections or dreams they had to inform, reveal or keep marching. I copied each chapter into its own document to work on in isolation, pulling it up to match the best I had so far; or if the book worked without it, I left it out. When each was a smooth whole that worked by itself, stating its own little goal at the beginning, moving to its own hook at the end, I added it back to the manuscript.

One unwitting advantage I'd given myself came from using a nickname on the cover page. I went by the nickname Pierre for years among friends, and didn't think twice about putting it on the manuscript. Then I found it was a switch that turned off a level of self-consciousness and lent distance to the work, as if it were somebody else's. Had my family name been there I could've been tied in psychological knots over the quality of the writing. I know it sounds simple but this can do your head in. When your first draft is complete and ready to improve, I recommend you add James Joyce to the header; then it's his work and you can tear it to shreds.

Following this chapter I include some steps towards structure. Maybe one day we'll keep them all in mind as we write, but for now I recommend making a whole pass through your draft for each of those steps. Don't stop for anything else, barely the odd word, as you skim through. After those seven passes it will be a different book. Then read it through and see how it travels. Trim it for speed, keep tightening here and there, spackle in new sentences to connect and smooth. And after that, make a pass to add poison, to loosen anything tightened too much, to roughen it back up a little, add any final wildest dreams, go the extra mile.

Then pass through it again, and again, skimming. If you skim fast and light it will play out its rhythm like a pianola and your eyes will tangle and stop on phrases that jar. Change them, then back up a page and start skimming again. If a phrase or word still jars after three passes, take the fucker out or reduce it to a simpler statement: 'No matter how hard we tried, the door remained firmly shut' to 'The door wouldn't budge.' Then move on. This part of the job is about decisions, don't stop to agonise. Make them like a soldier, and if in doubt, cut them out. By the time you've skimmed the work twenty times, smoothing and improving with each pass, you'll notice that only the same three or four things jar every time. You change them every time, then change them back. If the eye kept tangling on 'however', you changed it to 'nevertheless', and on the next pass changed it back to 'however', then back to 'nevertheless', then back to 'however'.

When those little tangles are all that's left, your work is finished.

This is how, at least the way I came to it, the work had two distinct seasons. The first one feverish and unrestrained, then this season more emblematic of cardigans and tea. Not that I own a cardigan, but my shoulders rounded and fell as if I did. A time of measured, tinkering thought, of sitting back, staring hard and scratching your head. A crossword puzzle. In a first draft, once you're blooded and flying on fatigue and adhesion to your pages – which can take a while – half your stress comes from fear of leaving the work and losing that flight to the cold light of day. But in the next season the job is always there waiting. It no longer flies, it sits in cold light, ready to be sculpted or chipped. You can sleep and come back to it, have good days and bad days, take one step forward and two back. But the thing is always there. Still, easier to improve than originate from scratch, which is what this technique is all about.

One analogy I've found to be true and worth keeping in mind: although there can be fast improvements all over a book, it won't gel into a single cohesive life right away. Keep going, keep faith, because it can follow the reductive dynamic of a slow meat stock. You boil it down for fifty hours, and, sure, it distils mathematically, you can see it reducing and growing richer hour by hour.

But flavour and texture don't gel until the last ten minutes.

Always simmer your work until then.

A story should have a beginning, a middle, and an end . . . but not necessarily in that order.

Jean-Luc Godard

26 FOUR STEPS TO STRUCTURE

Proportion

Beginning, middle and end: we always suspected those words were loaded. Obviously a story begins when we start it and ends when we stop; everything in between is middle, duh. But here's how those terms are loaded: they're about what happens at the borders between beginning and middle, and middle and end. We need the idea because when you dive off the jetty of your first page of work and swim across the hours, weeks or months it takes you, you only see unbroken ocean. There are no markers halfway. This is how it feels. Swimming out, often by night, no shore in sight and no guarantee that a shore is even there. And it occurs to you: how much of the swim is the beginning? When does it start to end? You first ask this when you feel yourself drowning.

A story travels, a reader will set out as we did to see where it goes. They won't tolerate drowning. It needs markers or they won't dip a toe into the book again. And not just chapter markers, something has to happen to our characters in the story. Creative freedom and originality aside, what we're up against is that people are not only taught to read but to *expect*; not only the spelling but the shape has to work; we're trained to hunt the curves of a classical story, and anything too weird defeats that programming. It's as if we're free to play whatever tune we like, but on an existing piano, just to throw another metaphor into the pot. It seems strange because we love the unexpected, we want to be surprised when we read, but in ways we can grasp. Otherwise it's too hard. Plus, if everything were surprising there would be no surprise. Anyway, we don't have readers, forget about them. This is still for us.

Bearing in mind that the truly beautiful is often strange in its proportions, the following approach to beginning, middle and end is the un-strange way to do them, a guideline to what has worked so far. This basic three-act structure comes from Aristotle, so there are warehouses full of academic pondering on it, and as much terminology as a cricket match. I'll dispense with all that here, we just want timber for our story, and this old chestnut is credited with framing many of the great stories of history. Our job may eventually be to surpass handed-down structures like this, but in the meantime, when you're feeling around in the dark for a sure-fire solution, this is it.

The proportions of a work are dictated by its drama. Shit happens in a story, and if you follow this scheme it happens in certain places, banging the tale out of its beginning into the middle, slapping it out of the middle to the end. In case it sounds artificial, the curious thing – and where academia has worn away many elbow patches – is that it does often resemble life. It goes back to the philosophy of human action, and I've also observed its forms in writing, fictional and biographical, from centuries ago. I've seen these shapes occurring naturally in tightly wound little cycles, in sprawling sagas, and in everyday anecdotes – so there is something of real nature in them, if only in the way we understand where they go.

This structure applies typically to drama and screenwriting, but it's good solid timber for any plot, all the stronger for catering to stricter dramatic arts. I fell into it because my protagonist Vernon Little referenced his life to movies, so it naturally followed that his book should resemble one. In the end nobody, that I know of, noticed the allegory; it seemed invisible and just kicked the story along. To gauge where the use of devices like these sits on a socio-political and commercial spectrum, put it this way: the more strictly you pull off these manoeuvres, the more readable your work will be. I don't add them to encourage blockbuster thinking, but if you're headed that way, these are the keys. As for the rest of us, it can be good sometimes to know what we're ignoring.

It looks like this:

Guideline proportions are simple – 1:2:1 – the middle is as long as beginning and end put together, or Acts 1 and 3 are each half the length of Act 2. Before looking at their dramatic functions, note some practical carpentry: Acts 1 and 3 should be faster, one whirling towards the middle, the other accelerating back out. In practical terms it means shorter chapters, shorter paragraphs, more dialogue, more action than reflection (i.e. more scene than sequel). Whereas Act 2 can slow down and dive deeper into the story, its chapters can be twice as long as in Acts 1 or 3, and with more reflection than action. This gives the work a speed curve, its motion reflects the story's pace in the same way that time seems to quicken and slow around events in real life.

The borders between acts are formed by plot-points, which are what really make a tale fly. These are turning points in the drama, reversals and setbacks spinning one Act into another on a new trajectory:

ACT 1

Act 1 sets up characters and their stomping grounds, also their values and the values of their world. The protagonist's ardent goal is stated early and unambiguously, and seeds are planted for the nature and scale of the shit he might face. As Kurt Vonnegut recommended, start the story as close to the ending as possible; meaning that if a plane is going to crash, start the act with screaming passengers. Towards the end of this act the protagonist faces an incident that requires him to respond. It should give rise to the story's big question: *will the character really achieve his goal?*

PLOT-POINT 1

The protagonist responds to that incident but his response defeats him in life-changing ways. This is a reversal of fortune, an insurmountable twist that seems to put the character's goal beyond reach. In *Vernon God Little* the first-act incident was Vernon being hauled off to jail. His response was to shout for help to the news cameraman Eulalio Ledesma. The plot-point was Ledesma turning out to be an enemy.

ACT 2

That turning point pits the protagonist against whatever forces it unleashes, in Vernon's case the media in the person of Lally Ledesma. Things get serious, Vernon faces defeat after defeat trying to chase his fading goal. Small triumphs only serve to lift his and our hopes before being dashed even harder. Note that action has to be organic, from visible cause and effect; obstacles don't appear out of nowhere, they happen as a result of the characters' manoeuvring. A principal cause of the protagonist's failure is that he doesn't yet have the keys to unlock his situation, be they self-knowledge or whatever enlightenment it will take to find a way out. His character grows and changes as a result of the pressures mounted against him, and his perception is changed by other characters. He grows self-aware. Still, by the end of this act the protagonist's goal appears hopeless.

PLOT-POINT 2

He gets the keys. Another reversal, new information, or a challenge so outrageous that he finds in his changed self the keys to new strength and stands up. In Vernon's case he had actually managed to escape during the second act; now he's recaptured to a jail where at the eleventh hour an older mentor gives him the idea for a solution.

ACT 3

The narrative flies to a climax, the accumulated tension of plot and subplots rises like a breaker before the protagonist as he mounts a do or die attempt on the goal. He might face another defeat, an anti-climax – but it serves to heighten tension and make his triumph all the sweeter when it comes. In the process of answering the story's main question – *will he actually achieve his goal?* – all subplots are resolved and mysteries revealed. He's a changed character. The end.

Add to this shape your control of fast and slow writing – action, including dialogue, is fast, and accelerates; reflective writing is a brake and slows – and they will set off a pumping action that makes the story breathe. The speed of that breathing is set by the measure of action to reflection. More action, less reflection – faster. More reflection, less action – slower. The next step in structure is to set this balance.

Before we take a gun and blast our damned pages.

There are three rules for writing a novel.
Unfortunately, no one knows what they are.

W. Somerset Maugham

27 FOUR STEPS TO STRUCTURE
Breathing

It's said that all writers are naive, but I drove myself crazy
with my first book. I was working from a feeling, chasing
something shapeless, and let the feeling take control of
the work. Although many first-draft ideas and sentences
made it into the book unchanged, all together they still
didn't add up to the feeling I wanted. They were fragments of it. If you saw the way my mind worked you'd
get an inkling of why so much needed figuring out with
a pencil: apart from the feeling I was trying to capture
I'd also decided the story had to have the nature of a
lime. Fucking shoot me. Not just any lime but a specific
one. I'd been roaming the streets and had brought home
this lime that looked like other limes but was special, its
perfume was unexpected and compelling. So it fixed in
my mind as a model for the work's nature. Try writing
a three-hundred-page lime if you want to drive yourself mad. Christ's sake. Among the things I identified to
deal with on this mission, to both capture the feeling and
make it like this one lime – which meantime I'd eaten
and couldn't even reference any more – the one that
confounded me was the fast and slow of the thing. As
I've said, action, conflict and dialogue are fast writing,
terse and simple. I flew through them as a reader: bang,
she fired, he ran. It was exciting writing and I started to

feel that the whole book would have to be like that to be exciting.

But then, without warning, something I'd written would prompt a chunk of slow writing, of reflection, philosophy, nostalgia; a dream sequence, a memory, some kind of inner searching. And I liked that writing, felt that it was probably the better work of the book. But it brought the action to a halt. Someone would fire a gun and I'd go off into a paragraph of fucking poetry before the bullet hit anyone. Still, I liked that poetry, it was doing my work, expressing the soul of the thing. So I went through a phase of toning down the action so that the poetry didn't seem slow, trying to harmonise them. But then the whole thing was too slow. I made a habit of reading the book from page one every time I sat down to it, and found that skimming it like that gave a good sense of its flow. But the fast/slow of it was killing me. Reading it through, I discovered that action has a breathless effect, it's like physical running, exciting but tiring, an inhalation. By comparison reflection is a long exhalation, time to catch your breath back. So the effect of fast and slow writing was of inhalation and exhalation, and what I was doing by pausing to put poetry amid the action was making the thing hyperventilate.

That was the key. A book that feels good to read, a book that's alive and healthy, has a respiratory cycle. It breathes in and out. Action is action and reflection is reflection and they come one after the other, not in between. It follows that too long a stretch of action kills the book by over-excitement. Too long a stretch of poetry puts it to sleep.

So after the three-act structure, the next level down was a respiratory cycle. I had to manage its breathing. I went to work setting that balance.

I did it nominally – that is, I set a ratio – which in the case of *Vernon God Little* was 2:1 action to reflection in Acts 1 and 3, and the reverse in Act 2. I wanted the book to clip along like the kid's life. These are bare guidelines, I didn't add or cull words just to fit the ratio, approximating it worked fine. Even in ragged proportions these structures become invisible, we don't realise we're breathing according to their speed; it just feels right.

To be clear: this is separate from rhythm, which comes from word placement, and sentence and paragraph length – this is big structure, it's the house we're building. It feels right when it breathes easily, you won't be able to put your finger on it.

So for proportion we have one long line marked in two places by plot-points; think of this as the line of the journey. Underneath it in parallel run any subplots, any stories within the story. If you draw this as a chart it can be useful to write the subplots under the chapters where they develop, to keep all the clues straight.

Then within it all, inside each chapter, a breathing structure. Action at the top, reflection flowing from that. So in my mind I could break each chapter in two: a fast part and a slow part, and that's where their respective writing went. By adjusting the length of these parts I could also control the overall speed of the book.

We can mix things up occasionally to break the routine – throw in a pair of all-action chapters back-to-back till lungs are bursting for breath, or let reflection lead to reflection in the depths of Act 2. But from now on we do it with awareness. The thing is alive and breathing.

Inside this structure comes another, the last one down. It explains how drama fits in, and shows how that drama is used to separate action and reflection into naturally occurring parts. I'm explaining all this summarily from the top down because it makes more practical sense; we can read Aristotle and confuse ourselves in our spare time. I also presume you're sat bleeding in front of some pages.

So this last structure down is the bestseller formula.

Just be gentle with it.

What is drama but life with the dull bits cut out.

Alfred Hitchcock

28 FOUR STEPS TO STRUCTURE
Drama

Our character Frank may only want to apply for a loan to open a pet shop. But he'll be turned down in chapter one, will approach his parents in chapter two but hear that their pension fund has just crashed, and in chapter three he'll take a new job only to find that his salary is calculated in benefits and not cash. The more dastardly his defeat, the more compelling the story will be: he goes to apply for the loan on the day of a bank robbery and is implicated in it, he finds his wife making out with the manager in the car park, etcetera. Thanks to us he'll struggle throughout the book, continually knocked down until the end, when he can throw off his chains and explode. To keep things interesting he might win a point or two along the way, but they only serve to make his defeat more crushing when it follows . . .

Here's the thing about this pearl of formula: a cycle is running through all of a protagonist's upheavals, one that I've seen in books from centuries ago, even biographies, probably without the formula being known to the author. Which suggests that it does resemble life, at least as the mind interprets it. This cyclic structure posits that people, and hence characters, in pursuing their goals collide with other people whose aims are at odds with theirs, and that a conflict ensues, often followed by a defeat which we deal with in certain ways every time. So the cycle forms two halves: one an active conflict and then a quandary, following which we devise a new angle of attack, decide to act on it, and set off again towards a new conflict.

The first half is action, the second half reflection.

What promotes page-turning in a book is just this:

	HOOK
Action:	GOAL
(Scene)	CONFLICT
	FAILURE
	DILEMMA
Reflection:	DECISION
(Sequel)	ACTION
	HOOK

The cycle fits neatly into a chapter, hence the hooks each end. It breaks down like this:

ACTION

This is the inward breath of a chapter or section. Fast, immediate writing where every word propels the story along.

A. Hook

A first sentence or paragraph to pull us into the chapter. If it's in the first chapter it needs to be a biggie and pull us into the book. My favourite first line is from Günter Grass's *The Tin Drum*: 'Granted: I'm an inmate in a mental institution.' It tells us that despite his position there's something big to say.

B. Goal

Somehow the chapter's goal has to be affirmed. It can be done obliquely, better still in the course of an action that moves the story along. It can also just be plainly stated: 'Today I'm approaching the bank for a loan.' This keeps the narrative pointed in the right direction and, done well, is one of the invisible markers that make a narrative flow without disturbing the experience of the story. If it's in the first chapter, the protagonist's goal for the whole book should be declared as soon as possible. Crafty writers bury it in the hook: 'The police didn't believe I was trying to open a pet shop.'

C. Conflict

Whatever the protagonist sets out to do runs into trouble. Conflict ensues. This is the action part of the chapter, fast-moving, shown and not told, its transactions best conveyed through dialogue.

D. Failure

The protagonist's efforts fail. The more decisively they fail, looking as if the game is over and the book must end, the more compelling the effect. This is where the bank manager turns out to be a prick, if not something more unexpected.

Slower writing. This is an exhalation and a stock-taking. Your poetic writing, your memories, quandaries, dream sequences and flashbacks go here.

E. Dilemma

It's all over. The protagonist's attempt has failed and he's left with the pieces. Here he takes stock of the mounting pressures and thinks up new avenues of attack. Should he go to another bank for the loan? To his parents?

F. Decision

As a result of his musing he decides what to try next.

G. Action

He picks himself up and takes a first step towards the next approach, if only by dialling a number, making a note or leaving the room.

H. Hook

The phone rings. A knock comes at the door. He notices something which casts the endeavour in a new light. Something begins to happen here that makes us want to move to the next chapter and find out. Once you get past the first chapter these hooks are like hook and eyelet: if the phone rings at the end of the chapter, the hook at the beginning of the next scene involving that character will be someone picking it up.

If you're writing a spy novel driven by plot, this is how it works. The formula is invisible to readers, they simply find the going easy and compelling, notwithstanding everything else that's in the book. As a loose procedure this can benefit most types of writing, even non-fiction, journalism and biography, by simply establishing where the fast and slow writing can go, and in what approximate order.

I include it here because I once spoke with final-year students in a creative writing degree who knew all the theory of writing but hadn't distilled it to any practical craft. One beautiful thing about writing: everything ever written is there to study with our own eyes. Look through some chapters of writers you admire. The markers will be there, more or less pumping the story along like this.

Here's an example of the structure in action. To see how much it seems to come from nature, at least human nature as we recall and tell our stories, this is a fragment from the late-eighteenth-century memoir of Jacques Casanova. I seriously doubt he considered formula as he wrote, and yet the whole seven-volume work, thousands of pages of it, is a chain of tight little cycles that follow the scheme above, a bunch of them per chapter. I don't suggest we cram so many cycles into our work, but he shows that we can. In this piece he writes of himself as a twelve-year-old in 1737, recounting his first play for a girl's love, in a doctor's house in Padua where he lodged. Bettina is the doctor's daughter:

This girl took at once my fancy without my knowing why, and little by little she kindled in my heart the first spark of a passion which afterwards became in me the ruling one.

Bang, he states a burning desire and we're hooked. Then a rival turns up and away we go: hook, goal, conflict, failure; dilemma, decision, action, hook. We can read him, as they say, like a book. I abbreviate the scene to its active points:

⌀⌀⌀

In the early part of autumn, the doctor received three new boarders; and one of them, who was fifteen years old, appeared to me in less than a month on very friendly terms with Bettina . . .

The antagonist Cordiani appears. Casanova acts on his goal:

. . . I composed a letter . . . My letter was, in my own estimation, a perfect masterpiece, and just the kind of epistle by which I was certain to conquer her very adoration, and to sink for ever the sun of Cordiani, whom I could not accept as the sort of being likely to make her hesitate for one instant in her choice between him and me. Half-an-hour after the receipt of my letter, she told me herself that the next morning she would pay me her usual visit . . .

It seems to have worked immediately:

. . . but I waited in vain. This conduct provoked me almost to madness . . .

But he's thwarted and forced to go to plan B:

. . . I therefore managed to tell Bettina that I would leave ajar the door of my room, and that I would wait for her as soon as everyone in the house had gone to bed. She promised to come . . . I was delighted at the idea that I had at last reached the moment so ardently desired.

The instant I was in my room I bolted the door and opened the one leading to the passage, so that Bettina should have only to push it in order to come in; I then put my light out, but did not undress. When we read of such situations in a romance we think they are exaggerated; they are not so . . .

Until midnight I waited without feeling much anxiety; but I heard the clock strike two, three, four o'clock in the morning without seeing Bettina; my blood began to boil, and I was soon in a state of furious rage.

Another defeat, another dilemma, another plan:

One hour before day-break, unable to master any longer my impatience, I made up my mind to go downstairs with bare feet, so as not to wake the dog, and to place myself at the bottom of the stairs within a yard of Bettina's door, which ought to have been opened if she had gone out of her room. I reached the door; it was closed, and as it could be locked only from inside I imagined that Bettina had fallen asleep . . . Overwhelmed with grief, and unable to take a decision, I sat down on the last step of the stairs; but at day-break, chilled, benumbed, shivering with cold, afraid that the servant would see me and would think I was mad, I determined to go back to my room.

Can things possibly get any worse?

I arise, but at that very moment I hear some noise in Bettina's room. Certain that I am going to see her, and hope lending me new strength, I draw nearer to the door. It opens; but instead of Bettina coming out I see Cordiani, who gives me such a furious kick in the stomach that I am thrown at a distance deep in the snow.

The length of a cycle like this in your work is a matter of its speed and timeline. I've seen the cycle repeated three and four times in a chapter, as with Casanova, whirring through defeats, and I've seen it spread across whole acts. For me, the length of a modern chapter is good for just one cycle, but they can also intermingle; as a story gathers depth, the cycle for one chapter can reach into the next and knock it off course, or they can run parallel in the lives of different characters. A whole barrel of monkeys.

The next step, key to using hooks and creating tension, is to alternate settings in a chequerboard throughout the story. Then the monkeys run amok.

A man can stand anything except a succession of ordinary days.

Johann Wolfgang von Goethe

29 FOUR STEPS TO STRUCTURE
Chequerboard

Hooks at the end of chapters are cliff-hangers, they're meant to leave us wondering what the hell will happen next. The better they are, the less we'll be able to put the story down. And in the armoury of cliff-hanging there's another tool of unfair advantage which involves changing scenes and settings in alternate chapters. It's built for a third-person voice but if you're crafty you can also make it work in first-person, or by using more than one first-person voice.

Say Frank is going to the bank for a loan. He goes, there's a conflict, the manager throws him out – and at the end of the chapter his phone rings. It could be good news. It could be bad news. We want to know what it is, we know it's there for a reason. But when we turn to the next chapter it starts with a hook for a different scene, a new setting, another character. We have to wait to find out who's on the phone. Maybe in the new scene we learn that his wife has been secretly saving a nest egg. Maybe she has thousands, nearly as much as Frank needs to open the shop. But because his pride never allowed him to admit that he needed a loan, she doesn't know about his plans. So the money's there unbeknownst to him; and his plan is going from failure to failure for want of money, unbeknownst to her. Maybe she then receives a desperate call from Kate, her best friend. Kate urgently needs money to bail her kid out of jail. Frank's wife peers between the curtains thinking that Frank must be on his way home. She has misgivings about bailing Kate's kid out – but before we learn if she lends the money or not, the chapter ends. Cliffhanger. Back to Frank answering the phone. It's the police. A kid has just been jailed who claims to have been on a job for Frank when a crime was committed. Back to the wife: she tells Kate that she'll accompany her to the police station and see what can be done – and so step by step our plot thickens through the chequerboard, the dramatic cycles of all three characters overlap and will soon converge with a bang. This kind of shit is fun to plot and write, although note that it's difficult to design in detail beforehand. The best ideas will come once you have a couple of characters going about their lives – don't have too many, even three is a workload because each has relationships with the other two, making for six connections between them. Relationships can quickly multiply and tangle – just as in life.

Grasp the subject, the words will follow.

Cato the Elder

30 DIALOGUE

'Is it the?'
  'I mean otherwise we'll go beforehand, and I mean.'
  'Um.'
  'I don't know about you but I mean.'
  'How do you want this?'
  'Like that thing with Adam.'
  'Oh, don't.'
  'Reminds me, you haven't done the hm.'

This is what transcribed conversation looks like. Who knows what they're saying. We hit a paradox when we try to write realistically, one that says it's not as easy as simply describing life: in real life people don't speak realistic dialogue. As writers we have to craft it. It's a trick. A crucial one because what characters say in a book can make or break it. Dialogue not only kicks the story along, hides and reveals facts, accelerates or hits brakes, causes or kills conflict – it makes things credible or incredible.

On top of that it has to make us forget we're reading it.

It took me a while to see that certain rules govern dialogue, and some were the opposite of what I expected. I found them out the hard way, but when I applied them their effect was immediate and I never looked back. If you can get dialogue under control, you're halfway home. Good practices look like this:

NATURAL IS UNNATURAL

Our programming as listeners and readers creates a need for technique in dialogue: listening and reading are two different things, as you discover when you try to write what you hear. At first I couldn't understand why the conversations around me wouldn't translate verbatim to a page; but a refraction effect applies, sentences strangely bend like light hitting water. If you've already embarrassed yourself writing dialogue, chances are it's because natural speech looks unnatural when written. Record someone and you'll hear how peppered with reversals, repetitions and omissions their speech is. In its quest for meaning, the brain filters that out and delivers us a packaged concept with all the debris removed, which is great – until you try to write it.

The way around this is economy; package the concept yourself as concisely as possible. As an exercise, start with the dialogue you want to write, then remove every third or fourth word, or cut the sentence by half. Try cutting it until the meaning no longer survives, then add back the one or two words that return the meaning. It's surprising how few words a sentence needs to do its job. We fly through dialogue, it's one of the pleasures of reading, it puts us at the heart of the action. Tight dialogue may look curt at first, but let it rest overnight and you'll see that economy looks natural, the brain sorts it out and keeps moving.

SHOW, DON'T TELL

This practice applies particularly to dialogue. Where it might be easier to describe an action or a setting in prose, we get more involved if our characters expose them in dialogue. For example, this might be an interesting enough piece of prose:

Then there was Barry, wearing his usual sour face. Rather than complain of the cold, or put on a jumper, he had a habit of drowning his food in salt, as he said this stimulated the body's temperature-regulating mechanisms. Of course, it was because he simply liked salt but was ashamed to admit it after warnings he'd received about his health. He usually froze at dinner to prop up this façade.

The dialogue below says the same thing, and makes us eavesdroppers:

'Pass the salt.' Barry looked away. 'Not a crime, is it? For the cold?'

'You make it sound like one,' said Ira. 'You could put on a jumper.'

'They say chillies regulate body temperature.' Sarah pushed the salt-shaker through a maze of bottles and glasses. 'And tea.'

Dan wiped his mouth: 'Tea regulates it by making you sweat. He's hardly going to sweat. Lucky if he's any fluids left, I've filled the shaker twice this week.'

'Not a bloody crime, is it?'

'They're your arteries. Ask us after you pop one.'

BEAT AROUND THE BUSH

Indirectness is one part of speech we should preserve. It's another secret that isn't obvious when you start out with dialogue, but if you listen to how we speak you'll note that much of what we say assumes that we know each other, and that we already know most of what we're going to say. More than this, much of our speech is just a cover – for barbs, for unasked questions, for things we don't want to deal with directly. This is all good in writing. It draws us in because it not only seems natural but gives us mysteries to unravel and suspicions to confirm that are as rewarding in books as in life; it engages. Your character John, for instance, in life or in a book, would never come out and say, 'Jane, I hold you and your absences responsible for the pressure on our marriage.' Instead, we would guess that tension from an exchange like this:

Jane clattered downstairs: 'I might be late home again.'
  'Could've sworn I left it around here.'
  'Feel free to ignore me.'
  'Works well enough for you.'

LET IT FLOW

Flowing dialogue has to be balanced with letting us know which character is speaking; but dialogue with too many 'he said(s)' and 'she said(s)' is irritating. It's a perennial challenge to clearly identify who's speaking without lumbering the exchange with repetitions. While the beginning of a dialogue should firmly show who speaks and who answers, if the conversation continues you'll need other tools to keep it natural and rhythmic. One of a new writer's first tries can be to substitute other words for 'said' – 'he guffawed', 'she tittered' – and while you can get away with a few substitutions – 'laughed John',

'Sally smiled' – they also multiply fast and wear thin. There are more elegant ways to identify speakers, and in longer dialogues you'll need them all. First, don't put every attribution at the end:

'By the time I left the pub I could barely see them,' said Lucas.

Instead try breaking sentences with them:

'By the time I left the pub,' said Lucas, 'I could barely see them.'

You develop a sense of rhythm skimming through your own dialogue, and that's when to try shifting attributions to see where they fit best. Better still, *attribute with action*; use the opportunity to show what Lucas is doing as he speaks:

'By the time I left the pub,' Lucas lifted the blind, 'I could barely see them.'

SPEECH TAGS

The sharpest tool in that armoury, the speech tag, kills attributions altogether. It consists of breaking the first rule just a little and adding in one of the grunts or tics we agreed to eliminate, making it a characteristic of one of the voices. Across the length of a story we come to know characters by their idiosyncrasies, whether beginning replies with 'hmm' or 'but' or 'well', or pronouncing things a certain way, or speaking without punctuation. The key is to pick one or two for each main character and lead some of their sentences with them. If Lucas has a habit of saying 'um', then when we see it we know he's the speaker. It means that only he can have that tic, and he can't share the tics of others. Don't overuse tags, wait till they're needed, at full stretch after all the other ploys have been used – but then, with a tag each, your characters can chat at length without stopping for a 'said Lucas'. Tags may seem awkward at first, but watch them grow more subtle as your characters settle into themselves.

These tips are quick to learn and have an immediate effect on the page, which can boost us along. In case you fall in love with dialogue, we live in the best time for dialogue-heavy books – because it's fast, and we're fast, and it makes us eavesdroppers. Pace excites, and dialogue is pace. Falling into good dialogue on page one can put us in your pocket.

The road to hell is paved with works-in-progress.

Philip Roth

31 DESKTOP

Your screen desktop can end up looking like a bombsite when a book is underway. Everyone has their manners when it comes to word-processing, but in case you're coming to this from scratch, here's some of what I do. It's not a designed system but a routine that grew organically as I began to write. It does the trick.

BEFORE
Whenever I get an idea for a story I create a new folder for it. I title a new document, put the idea down and leave it in that folder. Some ideas are just fragments, but occasionally one comes along with long enough legs for a book, or at least a story. Usually just a sentence explains what the idea is.

Whatever title I give that document, I add the word 'dump'; and that's where I save anything else that comes to me with reference to that idea. It's an ideas dump and works like a magnet attracting filings to itself, which in turn sets up a natural system where some dumps grow more than others; an indicator of which book might be next on its feet. My works folder currently has twenty-five sub-folders that are all ideas. Some are no more than titles that trigger the idea. But others have a full idea inside them which over time attracts more notes. Whenever I bump into something relevant to one of the ideas, I add the note to that document. Some are now pages long, and some have never attracted a thing – although I like them still, and their time might yet come.

The dump with the most notes in it is the one I'll work on next. Like a bear waking from hibernation, a document's activity will increase at a certain point as its idea starts pulling in notes from the world around it, filling itself out. Then you know it's getting ready to go, its time has come. As soon as we declare the job underway, our bias and filtration systems start converting everyday experiences into angles for that story, and after that, dumps can grow to a hundred pages or more. They're also where to scribble whole wild passages in first draft when the spirit takes you. They're a genesis.

DURING

When I start a new work, I create a title document which will be the first draft, formatting it with double-spaced Times New Roman 12-point. From this moment the dump also serves for things I cut out of the main work, failed experiments and so on, but which have something in them that could be useful later, or elsewhere in some other work. After a few books you can end up with a novel's length of material in dumps, which can one day re-inspire you with fresh angles from times you'd forgotten. These documents are your sandpit, your wider workspace, a kind of external brain; back them up religiously as you go along. The trick with writing is to not physically delete all but the worst shit – just dump it out of your draft and label the fragment for reference.

Whenever you lift something from the dump to the book, leave the original text in the dump and highlight it in red so you know what's been used and what's still virgin. Along with the first-draft document and dump, I also create a patch document, a kind of pre-dump, a short-term parking document for when you're shifting blocks of text around, moving chapters or trying something out. Whenever you want to see if a chapter works just as well without a chunk of writing, cut that part out to the patch document and read the thing through without it. If it survives well enough without the chunk, move it to the dump. If you're unsure, it can stay in the patch until later. I sometimes end up with two or three patches on the go.

Another document to create and label for prominence is a checklist. Whatever else you put in it, it should warn you to read through all dumps and patches before finishing the work. It should also remind you to spell-check. It's easy to be swept up in a work's finale, but by then your head is crammed full of shit to remember. You can keep your mental cache clear by adding notes to yourself in the checklist: to remind you that you planted a condom in a character's pocket in chapter one, or need to tie up a subplot between the Johnsons. Make sure the checklist stays prominent in whatever main folder you use. I label mine 'A CHECKLIST' to keep it on top of the file tree.

When your first draft is written, another pair of new documents is useful. I label mine like cinema reels, 'A-Roll' and 'B-Roll', and extract whole chapters to them one at a time to work on in isolation. Often I'll only use the A-Roll, but if a chapter is symbiotic in its action with another, I can extract both and work on them as individual documents. As with surgery, it helps to isolate your patient and to work on a single whole, which also draws your attention to the smooth beginning and ending of a chapter. After a chapter is polished by itself, I save it again in its own document, which leads to another folder full of individual chapters; it can be an easier way to access them than skipping through a three-hundred-page typescript. I used to build codes into my first draft, macros to skip to chapters and sections I'd bookmarked, but current security programs don't like documents with embedded code. So for now I keep my pages clean of code and just have a folder full of numbered chapters. The challenge once they're separated is to polish each one up to the level of the chapter you're happiest with so far. Once each one shines by itself, I create a new document which is the final draft, and copy all the chapters in one by one. This is the most rewarding job of all: you've built and polished all your components and now assemble them into an engine and start it running.

The beautiful thing about a book: once it runs it will never stop.

AFTER

Once the thing is done, all your documents are an archive. I make sure the final draft is in the main folder by itself for later reference, or to edit from; everything else gets moved to the archive. At this point the patch and A-Roll documents should be empty, everything either in the dump or in the book.

Then back it all up, mix a stiff drink, and try to focus more than a yard away again

Art is science made clear.

Jean Cocteau

Postscript AHEAD

Suppose you were to go to sleep tonight and not wake up for twenty-five years. What would the world be like then? This book tells you what it *could* be like. It has two main distinctions from other works which hazard a picture of the future: first, most of its readers will be alive to see the world; second, at the end of the book the author details the scientific discoveries and inventions, the developments and trends on which his predictions are based, and he furnishes ample evidence in the form of some startling photographs of laboratory experiments, models, and prototypes from a number of countries. Thus the book is no idle speculation – it is mainly based on fact.

Waking after having spent the intervening years in deep-freeze hibernation, he describes the world he sees as any reporter would portray some hitherto unknown country. It is a strange world, much better than our pessimistic prophets assume, but not without its peculiar problems and difficulties. War is a thing of the past, and a benevolent though somewhat bureaucratic World Government is in charge of mankind's fate, while a very rich scientific foundation suggests and backs new developments. Instead of wasting their resources on armaments, the nations have succeeded in ending poverty; as a result, racial and religious prejudices have largely disappeared.

India is the industrial giant of Asia, and the Sahara is irrigated to become the world's fruit garden. Helicopters are as common as cars today, and nuclear power, tapped by the 'atomic battery' system, has changed the face of the 'under-developed' areas. Monorail trains and fast passenger submarines have been introduced, new foods developed, and the 'killer' diseases conquered – the expectation of life for a child born then is a hundred and twenty years. With almost complete automation, there is a twenty-four-hour week. Pedestrian roads at first-floor level have eased the traffic problems of the big cities. A daily 'rain hour', choosing marriage partners by TV, rooms adjustable for size and shape, electronic coloured light from the walls, shopping by pneumatic tube, hypnotic sleep as a psycho-therapeutic treatment, newspapers printed at home by facsimile-reproduction – it is a brave and amazing new world, but a completely plausible one. The author ends his report with the first voyage to the moon via the space station.

These were jacket notes from Egon Larsen's 1957 book *You'll See*, subtitled: *Report from the Future*. The time he was looking forward to was 1982.

So much for that. We did eventually get the marriage-partner-by-TV thing, and newspapers by facsimile-reproduction. But note the one glaring omission from his equation: *our fucking species*. His model presumed that given the right tools and conditions, such as wealth, we'd do something humane with them.

It's quaint to think that we could so recently find around us the evidence to predict that our race would grow through technology and be liberated from the ignorance and chaos which is so profitable and so loved by us all. Today we're in no such danger of being tricked.

Except, obviously, with powerful music, strong drink and ecstasy.

You can be an optimist or a pessimist about where we're going, but these last words are about where we are. In terms of writing characters it doesn't matter where we are unless you're prone to activism; whether you write an Ancient Egyptian romance, a Tudor saga or a contemporary novel, the characters are identical, which is to say unimproved humans with the same quirks as ever. Perhaps the only marked difference today is fallout from individualism, so committed relationships like marriage are as onerous as becoming Amish used to be.

We started this discussion in the gap between conceptual ideal and existential chaos, and we should finish there. For this last chapter, a helicopter view before we skulk back into our holes, we should take stock of what's been happening over the horizon. One thing on the radar is the gradual collapse of the nation state, a process underway for decades, although no one's talking about it. The idea to bind different societies into single political territories is pretty recent and didn't last long. Borders and the notion of borders have been surpassed, we permeate them physically and electronically now as a matter of routine. Political territory has been the cause of most conflict over the last century, including both world wars, the likes of which had never happened before in history. What we might take from it is that we've outgrown the way we govern ourselves; our ideas failed just as Larsen's predictions failed, for not taking human nature into account – and I don't think human nature is hopeless, it can be pretty cool unless you try to make it fit theories. Another broader terrain, now the elephant in the room, is the gap itself between ideal and chaos. It escaped no one that the gap is the home of psychology – another recent idea – and that psychology is both a tool and a weapon. So we live in increasingly studied psychological zones now mastered for profit. The gap has been bought like a rental property with us in it, the genius of which is that it's our own headspace, with no immune system, so our feeding on its manufactured ideas still makes us feel like agents of free will, defining our individuality.

We will step from this book to that feed-trough. We can feed there happily enough, it sells drinks and sex, 'we no complain'. Just the idea of it pisses us off, but it pisses us off over a cocktail, so what can we say? As writers we just need to be aware of the dynamic, and maybe think about what comes next – because there'll soon enough come a next where we and our haircuts, hand signals, tattoos, sentimentality and save-the-day spirit will look as dated and stupid as advertisements on black-and-white TV.

The biggest change to human terrain is something Larsen got dead right. What's pertinent about his book isn't the predictions, but a sense of the environment around him, a feeling that things were brewing fast. He could tell they were going to explode, and they did explode: the only predictable curve in the last seventy years has been technological improvement. So we live in a time when change is not only fast but we're aware of it being fast. That never happened before. A farmer in history could be certain that his descendants would face the same conditions and use the same tools as he had. Aside from transient upheavals, widespread essential change was never a feature of life, in the sense that it could be noticed within a lifespan. For most of history, basic change wouldn't have been noticed by someone who lived a thousand years – history as lived appeared static. Now, 2.6 million years after we started making tools, the last 0.016 per cent of our history has produced the most change, an exponential curve turning vertical. It's why I keep saying 'a recent idea' to anything less than a couple of centuries old. That change is young, its paint is still wet. And it's still external, due to mechanisation and its effects, it hasn't really changed humans except to make the affluent fat – and by affluent I mean anyone who shits in good drinking water.

As for us we remain greedy and vain, and the ideology behind current change has made an engine of those traits. As observers we may sense that things aren't right, but current logic seems to find space for them – provided they're profitable.

But then look at this: equal to the explosion in change is an explosion in arts, media and music. Once discouraged in excess, entertainment and music now ride shotgun, we devour them, we plough with them, drive with them, eat with them, chill with them, make love with them, travel with them and create them for others. We walk around in our own little worlds of them. And so, going back to the beginning, I pondered: the taste in my childhood mouth ended up being a taste of bad experience from the gap, of distortions and lies. Looking into it I found its mothership, the gap between chaos and ideal, and after a while that tasted wrong as well. As if it was widening too fast for us to finesse any more, and towards places we hadn't aimed for, and couldn't know. As if this change wasn't simply progress but a culmination, one we were unprepared for, and in the new light of which we didn't know who to be or where to stand.

The feeling I pumped into my first novel was a shout at distortions of value as the gap stretched around us, distortions I'd tasted before. And plenty of people got that shout, there are other shouters out there with the same taste in their mouths. So adding it all up, it hit me – maybe art rises to deal with specific challenges. The current deluge of fictional arts and media might make this sense: *science can't teach chaos.*

Science can't predict or explain the accidents of reciprocal human change. Beyond some colours on a brain scan it has no power over human accidents, and hence no interest. The exclusive agents of the intuitive and the unspeakable are the arts. And here we are flocking to them, wallpapering our lives with rehearsed human outcomes by proxy, as humanity grows mysterious around us.

There's our workspace as writers. There's our mandate – who the fuck are we now, in what I predict is a century of psychology and conflict? It doesn't matter how technology comes to bear on it, technology is predictable. Its power, its wealth, is boring. It's supposed to be a tool, not the main game. And in the end whose life poses bigger questions: the programmer with the private jet or the girl whose palms bleed at Easter? A century changed us and much of that change lies in ways to scrutinise ourselves, which makes you think we don't even know who we're looking at any more. Who are we now? When our horse-manship, our mothering, our knowledge of the land, our integrity, our far-sightedness, our meekness and even our laptop don't count any more? (I only claim to possess the laptop.) Our unconscious has to rehouse personality against a vertical curve of change. We can't count on the neighbours any more, the news is bullshit and the farm has long been sold; but maybe we read, listen and watch our way to an adjustment through a higher language of impressions, beyond the reach of laboratories and governments. Maybe we're writing, playing, singing and acting our way out. Technology can't do what humans do. Whatever it is that we do, we should do it now in earnest. If art is the gap's boatman, its job now grows critical: because it alone addresses our humanity.

And we're going to need some of that.

At least according to this seamless conceptual model.

Good luck!

Appendix

QUICK GUIDE

BATS AND MICE

MEMORY
Wherever you are when you first ponder a thought or question, physically go back there to continue pondering or to remember it again. Memory seems to sit where you leave it.

UPS AND DOWNS
A logical, if unexpected practical phenomenon: feeling exceptionally crap about yourself will make you unable to see good writing, and feeling elated will blind you to crap. Compensate for this one; the key is to lay the work down and look again later.

BAD FEELING
Bad feeling in this game is a horse we have to ride. If you sit down to write and spend nine hours on four words that you don't like, you leave disgusted with yourself, reluctant to return to the page. Develop a position separate from the feeling – above it. Watch it, note it, but like passing weather. Feelings aren't us, we're the ones watching them. And know that it contributed some rocket fuel to spend later. Tough it out, accept it, and keep going back. One good habit to foster: try to leave the work when you're still happy with it.

CLAUSES AND LISTS

A gremlin: for some reason when a sentence has two or three clauses, or lists two or three things, I often put them down backwards. For example: 'Won't they see it? Do they live in the building?' should be: 'Do they live in the building? Won't they see it?' It's weird, I can't account for it, but make a note to return to multiples like this and check them again. On closer inspection you can find that they read better in reverse.

MAGIC NUMBER

It turned out to be three, after all. Any set of words or phrases in a list, as in separated by commas, seems to work best in sets of three. 'He was spitting, howling, raging with it.' That is if you have to use more than one expression at all.

WRITE FROM A DISTANCE

I wrote a novel set in Texas from a flat in London, a novel set in the Caucasus from a house in Ireland, a novel set in Berlin from a house in England; but I knew all the places I wrote about. Problem is, those places don't seem to become useful as written settings until you've left them behind and they distil to essential details in your mind. There's too much of them to filter when you're sat in the middle, and their essential light is somehow stronger when you look back. The possible moral: come back from China to write about China.

MINDSET

This is a job where it's better to be lucky than intelligent. Your mind can obsess over things, not even valid ones, and mess them up, whereas your desire knows what it wants to say. Luck comes from conquering risk, and the risks in this game are in our heads. Learn to put the head aside for a while.

MUSES

Every stage of a work, every character and chapter can have its own muse with its own intelligence. That must be why it takes time for the thing to grow, and why we should keep faith. It's also as if every mood and season we live through while writing corresponds to a particular part of a book, a domain of that muse. So if you find yourself struggling with one section, find another with a more agreeable climate for the day. Between them all: you'll get there.

CHAPTERS IN MIND-BITES

Suck them up or stick them up.

1

Nothing is as it seems.
Show what really is.

2

We more easily believe
an idea than a fact.

So do our characters.

3

The taste in your mouth
is ultimately what you're
writing out.

Whether you know what it is
or not: trust it.

4

What would you write
if you weren't afraid?

Write that.

5

The boy stood
on the burning deck.

And then?

6

'The tigers have
found me,
and I do not care.'

7

PUNCH.

Don't aim for the target,
aim beyond it.

(8)

It's far easier to improve crap than to originate brilliance.

Love crap.

9

Ideas
attract
their
own
furniture.

10

Thomas Wolfe
had to stand naked
fondling his genitals
in order to write well.

Do what you
have to do.

Eccentricities make characters.

All that we appear to be
is cover for a deeper,
sometimes opposite truth.

Uncover it in writing.

Headfucks are symptoms
of an underlying mass.

We don't lose it,
we move it.

Conflict.

Trap your characters
till they work it out.

Mystery.

The answer should seem
inevitable, looking back.

Events don't arise from
purposeful steps.

They arise from walking through
accidents.

17

The human immune system
is at its most effective
against the ideas of others.

18

Reality is stricter
in books.

A piano can't
just fall on
someone's head.

19

Symbols:
the gloves we use
to pat spiders.

Weakness:
heroes have it most.

21

Protagonists
don't simply want
something badly.

They burn for it.

22

Antagonists
aren't just bad.

They're beyond help.

23

Good writing by
modern standards
is an economical
chain of vivid
suggestions.

Write in a reckless fever.
Rewrite in a cardigan.

A fifty-two-hour meat stock
doesn't gel till the
last ten minutes.

Simmer your work
until then.

(26)

Act 1	Act 2	Act 3
Setup	*Confrontation*	*Resolution*

Plot-point 1   Plot-point 2

BREATHE:
action,
reflection,
action,
reflection,
action,
reflection.

28

Action: (Scene)	HOOK GOAL CONFLICT FAILURE
Reflection: (Sequel)	DILEMMA DECISION ACTION HOOK

Chequerboard.

Don't move from the chapter
where the protagonist hangs
from a cliff to the chapter
where she falls. Go to her friend's
house, push her to a cliff as well.

Real dialogue isn't
natural in writing.

Make it economical,
and beat around
the bush.

31

Writing down an
idea for a story
is like
planting its seed.

A shitstorm looms.

Get writing.

With the permission of certain reprobates, a call to arms written for *The MEATliquor Chronicles.*

THE BOOK

The book is an end in itself. Nobody can like or dislike us because of opening it. They can tweet it out their ass. The book never needs upgrading. It doesn't self-lock. You agree no terms to buy it. You untick no box, open no account, sign no contract, receive no mail, reveal no whereabouts. Nobody will come in a year's time to make you pay for it again. It is a universe which you carry in your hand and open at the speed of your nature, again and again, for ever. It belongs only to you and is under your control. It has a smell, a texture, a colour, a style, and three organic dimensions. It teaches of, and for, and against all the things you choose it to, and is a human right whose loss would be an end to freedom. Because when every battery is in enemy hands, and all our little screens are dead – it will speak for you a thousand years more, and wear your stains upon it.

Stain this book.

IN CASE OF PUBLISHING

Publishing	*English*
'Good'	Crap
'Very Good'	Meh
'Extravagantly Good'	OK
'Brilliant'	Good
'Miraculous'	Brilliant
'Unique'	Bizarre
'Genius'	WTF?
'Excited'	When can I see some pages?
'Can't wait to catch up'	When can I see some pages?
'A drink on Tuesday?'	Show me some pages
'It's Dan's launch, he'd love to see you'	Show me some pages
'Sarah was just asking how you were'	Show me some fucking pages
'Been too long between drinks'	Where are those fucking pages?
'Thrilled'	They better be amazing after all this
'We've a lot riding on this'	Give it a happy ending
'But do we leave him in the right place?'	Give it a happy fucking ending
'It won't go unnoticed'	Plenty more where you came from